Defeating Depression

A Guide for Depressed People and their Families

C.A.H. Watts O.B.E., M.D.

THORSONS

THORSONS PUBLISHERS LIMITED
Wellingborough, Northamptonshire

First published 1980
Second Impression 1981

ISBN 0 7225 0574 4 (hardback)
ISBN 0 7225 0572 8 (paperback)

Photoset by
Specialised Offset Services Limited, Liverpool
and printed in Great Britain by
Weatherby Woolnough, Wellingborough, Northants, England

Contents

Acknowledgements

I must express my sincere thanks to Miss G.M. Axton, who was a great help to me in the writing of Chapter Four. I am also, as always, deeply indebted to my wife, Dr Betty Watts, who is virtually a co-author of this book.

Note

Though all the cases referred to in this book are real the names used are entirely fictitious.

Introduction

I had been qualified for some six years before the outbreak of the Second World War. During that time I learned that there were large numbers of emotional problems in general practice, and I realized only too well how defective my knowledge was on this subject. I joined the armed forces in 1940, and in 1944 the authorities asked for volunteers to attend a course on psychiatry in an army neuro-psychiatric hospital. I jumped at the idea, and the result was that I worked at the institution for a whole year. I realized that here was my opportunity to learn more on this important subject, which I felt could play a sizeable part in the practice of ordinary everyday medicine, though I never had any intention of abandoning general practice for psychiatry.

Thus, when the war was over, I started once again to practise as a family doctor in a rural area of Leicestershire. I discovered that depressive disorders of all kinds were extremely common, and for the past thirty-three years this subject has been my special interest.

Depression is indeed, a very common problem, and yet it is so often misunderstood and unrecognized by the community at large, and this includes some of the professionals in the caring services. When I was invited to write this book, with the aim of helping both patients and their families, I was very pleased to accept the challenge. The idea was to describe the various depressive illnesses, and to say what can be done to help the patient. Today depression is a treatable illness. I make no apologies for repeating this phrase again and again, because it is so important for the public to realize what can be done to help the depressed person.

Throughout the book I have generally referred to the patient as if she were a woman, and the therapist a male. There are of course many male melancholics, but it makes for easier reading if one can get away from the need of having to use the terms 'he' or 'she' constantly.

When I started my career as a medical writer in 1940, some forgotten mentor once told me that any article on any subject, no matter how complex it might be, should be intelligible to the average reader. This is what I have tried to do in this book. A few technical terms are inevitable, but these have been kept to a minimum, and there is a short glossary of them at the end of the book which defines those that have been used.

Chapter 1
What is Depression?

Mrs Adams was a woman of thirty-one when she came to see me. I had not seen her before, and she was a shy and diffident person. She complained of headaches and vague symptoms, and she told me that she had never really felt well since the birth of her second daughter some two years before.

She sat on the edge of her seat and gazed at the floor while she twisted her handkerchief into knots. When I remarked that she looked a little tense, she burst into tears, and kept trying to apologize between her sobs, saying that she felt so stupid and feeble.

When she had been taken along to an examination cubicle by the nurse I was able to have a word with the husband. He told me that he was very puzzled by her, and that it was only with the greatest difficulty he had persuaded her to come and see me. He went on to admit that at times he himself felt at the end of his tether; he knew that she was ill but could not make out what was wrong, nor why she was so reluctant to seek help.

This is a very common story. Many people who are depressed are perplexed and confused by their feelings. They cannot understand themselves, and they do not expect anyone else to understand them either. If, in a weak moment, the depressed housewife tries to explain to a friend how she feels, she is soon aware that her confidant is not really 'with her' any more and is completely at a loss as to what to say or advise. In the end, the sympathizer usually takes refuge in suggesting that she must pull herself together, get out more, and stop dwelling on how she feels. In general she tries to jolly the melancholic out of her low mood.

Unfortunately this attitude has quite the reverse effect as the depressed person can do none of these things. She has tried to snap out of it over and over again, and when her effort has been unsuccessful she has felt more feeble and miserable than before. This kind of difficulty in communication with a close friend does not encourage her to try and talk to her own doctor, and there are other factors which add to her diffidence.

Often she thinks that the trouble is in some way her own fault. She feels that she has failed her husband, and is only too conscious that she has let herself go both in appearance and in the standard of her house work. She blames herself and does not appreciate that she is ill, and so she remains reluctant to waste the busy doctor's time.

The experience of depression is also hard to describe, and the victim may well be at a loss as to what to tell the doctor. One patient told me she wished she had measles so that she could show me the rash. Another said she knew that there was nothing wrong with her organs, it was what held her together that was missing. Some people are convinced from the start that their condition is hopeless; that nobody can help them, and, so they argue, a medical consultation is fruitless.

All these peculiar feelings – the bewilderment, the sense of inadequacy and hopelessness, the inability to describe just how one does feel – are in fact typical symptoms of depression. They are not only disconcerting: they are misleading and very unfortunate, because *today depression is a treatable illness*.

What is Mental Depression?
To some extent, we all experience depression. The man who dents the wing of his car on the gatepost feels depressed; he has lost face as a driver, it is going to cost a lot of money to repair the car, and he is likely to be without transport for several days. With a huge load of grubby clothes in front of her, the housewife who finds her washing machine has broken down and has no hope of any repairs for a week similarly has every right to feel pretty desperate and miserable.

These are, however, minor upsets in life compared with other things like the impact of serious illness, as when the wage earner has a coronary thrombosis, or when the woman of the house has a stroke which puts her completely out of action. The traumatic situation need not, of course, involve illness. It can occur when the breadwinner is thrown out of work, or when the family has to be uprooted to live in a different part of the country, or even the world. It happens when the partners of a marriage realize that they are drifting apart, and seem quite unable to rectify the rift. Perhaps the most painful situation of all is when there is a sudden and unexpected calamity, as when some member of the family is killed in a road accident.

Some of these incidents are, of course, inevitable at some time in life, and they produce feelings of irritation, frustration, despair or sadness. But these reactions are not necessarily depressive in a medical sense. The actual illness of depression is something much more profound. My definition of such a depression is *the lowering of physical and mental vitality to the point of distress*. The victim not only feels low and miserable: she is also physically disabled.

The symptoms of this pathological type of depression are many and variable, but one of the earliest is certainly a falling-off of energy. It takes the greatest effort to carry on with a normal routine, and sometimes the breakdown is so overwhelming that the depressive can virtually do no worthwhile work. When she wakes in the morning, she wonders how she will manage to get through the day. She looks at the stairs and they appear as an insuperable obstacle: however can she climb to the top? The keen gardener goes outside one bright spring morning to do some work. He realizes with regret that the beauty of the scene is lost on him; he just cannot appreciate it as he should. It takes him half an hour to collect his tools, and then he is only capable of pottering about. Even this exhausts him, and the prospect of all the work ahead appals him.

Anxiety

Another common symptom of depression is anxiety. This can be well founded, but it is often spurious. The woman who is depressed because her husband has been diagnosed as having lung cancer has every reason to be worried. She feels he is doomed, and yet faced with this huge problem she may not be able to discuss it frankly with him in the way she has always shared difficulties with him in the past. As the fit member of the pair she tends to be overwhelmed by an extra share of responsibility. She now has to see that the bills are paid, and it is she who is accountable for the family discipline. Finally, as he is only on sick pay, she may well be worried to death over managing the family finances.

On the other hand, the patient's anxiety may have no rational basis. Cancer phobia is an example of this phenomenon. The man who imagines he has a growth in his throat, in spite of every reassurance from his G.P. and an expert consultant, tends to be intensely worried all the time. Most of us, when we fall ill, are inclined to fear the worst. If we get a cold we are contracting influenza; a pain in the chest means heart disease, and an attack of diarrhoea suggests a bowel growth. Doctors are probably worse at this kind of thing than other people, as they are well acquainted with so many horrible diseases. I remember when one of my children had glandular fever that I was convinced he had leucaemia, and for a week I was extremely distressed. Foolishly I did not get advice from a colleague because I felt that if indeed he had leucaemia, nothing anyone could do would help him.*

In the great majority of such situations, once the symptom has improved, we lose the fear, but in a minority of people it remains and becomes intensified, and defies all reassurance.

Other depressed patients suffer from what is called free floating anxiety. The victim feels tense and worried, but has no physical symptom on which to lay the blame: no chest pain to suggest a bad heart; no digestive symptoms to make her think of cancer. This type of patient may well conclude that the feelings are evidence that she is going out of her mind, and this thought in turn intensifies the state of tension. These spurious illogical forms of anxiety can be far more intense and frightening than the worry which accompanies some environmental disaster, and this is a typical feature of

* Childhood leucaemia is now a curable disease in many cases.

melancholia. A consultant physician who had had a great deal of experience in psychiatry, was quite shattered when he himself became depressed. Like so many victims, it was a long time before he realized he was in fact ill. He described the experience as a period of unspeakable agony, greyness and *anxiety*, the latter being far more terrifying than the simple anxieties of every day life.

Insomnia and Moodiness

Some upset of the sleep rhythm is inevitable in the melancholic. The type of insomnia can vary. The most common form is to wake in the early hours of the morning, and once aroused the patient lies in bed brooding, dreading the approach of yet another day. Some, with a predominance of anxiety, have difficulty in falling asleep, and others dread going to bed because their slumbers are so frequently broken by bad dreams. A minority sleep too heavily, and no matter how long they stay in bed, they wake up unrefreshed and exhausted.

Another disconcerting symptom is a marked variation in the mood pattern. The sort of thing that happens is that the patient feels ghastly in the mornings, as though suffering from a bad hangover; there is improvement as the day goes on, and by nightfall the patient is reasonably well. This alternation of mood, of feeling horrible at one time and almost normal a few hours later, can be most distressing as it amounts to a constant swing from fear to hope, and then back again to fear. It can also be a factor that keeps the patient away from the doctor. When she feels ill, she just has not the energy or drive to get in touch with him, and in a good mood she persuades herself that she is getting better and that she does not need to worry him.

Enough has now been said, I hope, to make it clear that there are two distinct types of depression. There are the low moods we all experience in the rough and tumble of life, the emotional 'downs' we are able to work through in a matter of hours or days without too much difficulty; and there is another form of melancholia which is far more severe and disabling, and which lasts a great deal longer. Furthermore, its victims cannot talk themselves out of the situation. It can be all-pervading, so that nothing can relieve the misery. These severe depressions form a group of genuine illnesses well known to the medical profession, and it is these conditions I am now going to describe and elaborate. In studying and observing their patients, doctors have been able to see that there are in fact different kinds of melancholia which have been named *reactive, symptomatic*, and *endogenous* depression. For reasons I will consider later, I prefer to call the last type a *primary endogenous depression*.

Reactive Depression

By far the most common form of melancholic illness is the reactive depression. This happens when the individual is completely bowled over by 'the slings and arrows of outrageous fortune'. It is indeed an extension of the normal everyday depression. Many people learn to cope remarkably well with trying situations, but we all have a breaking point, and some are more vulnerable than others. When disaster is piled on disaster, or some new and different strain is introduced, a depressive illness can emerge, and the sort of thing that can happen is well illustrated by the following case history.

Mrs Brown had been evacuated to our village from Coventry after that city had been devastated by the 1940 air raid. At first she was relieved to get away alive with her two children from the shambles of her native town, but this did mean leaving her home territory and all her friends. Her husband was away serving in the army. In spite of being in a rather lonely position, she integrated well into the local community and managed to adapt herself to a new way of life. She found herself living in the smallest of country cottages under most primitive conditions. She was helped to survive and put on a brave face, as there was a war on, and she was upheld by the *esprit de corps* which sustained so many.

In 1946, the war being over, her husband was discharged from the army and joined her, and she was soon expecting another baby. She then became very depressed. A number of factors contributed to this breakdown. They were now uncomfortably overcrowded in the cottage, and when the baby arrived things would be even worse. The pregnancy itself could have been an added strain. Above all, she was convinced that the town hall authorities in Coventry would have forgotten her after such a long absence, and she was sure that the family would never return to her native city.

Applications were made to the city council and long intimidating forms were completed, but all in all, as the weeks rolled by, she felt there was no hope. She had ceased to find any satisfaction in rural activities. I saw a good deal of her at counselling sessions, but nothing helped her. She admitted that she had a great deal to be thankful for, but this idea failed to comfort her and she remained tearful and miserable. Then, much to our surprise, she was offered a council house back in Coventry, and her depression rapidly cleared. She wrote to me six months later, after she had had her baby, to thank me for my help, and to say that she had made a complete recovery.

Unfortunately, there are many reactive depressions which cannot be sorted out quite so easily. The woman who is depressed because her husband has gone off with another woman is faced with an apparently insoluble problem. Such cases often need a counsellor to help them to reach some compromise, so that they can come to terms with the problem.

I served with the South African Forces during the last war and fighting with us were several anti-Nazi Germans. One such airman came under my care, an air force pilot called Lieutenant Hartmann. He had had a rough time during his operational flying in Italy; he had suffered a nervous breakdown and had been evacuated to the hospital in which I worked. He was a tall, good-looking young man of twenty-three, but he felt desperately ashamed of himself and was constantly in tears. He was convinced that he had let the side down, and felt an utter failure.

The background showed that both his parents were strong supporters of the Hitler regime. While he had respected their views, he did not agree with them. He had compromised by waiting until he was twenty-one before joining the South African Air Force. This had meant a rift with his family, and although he had written letters home he had never received any replies. Because of his emotional upset, he felt he could never face them again. He despised himself for being so feeble and lacking in self control. He felt, too, he had fallen down on his job, an undertaking his parents had made clear he should never have accepted. He had defied them, and had been proved foolish. He could imagine their disgust if he started blubbering in front of them. This young man in his own eyes had lost all his self respect, and he needed help to achieve its recovery.

I listened to his story with sympathy, and I pointed out that far from acting foolishly or on impulse, he had given great thought to his decisions, that he had in fact been considerate towards his parents and, in my view, correct in his motives. His file showed that he had an excellent service record, and it was pointed out to him that the peculiar situation at home had added enormously to his stress.

His was not an unusual type of illness among service men. There were many like him to whom he could talk in the officers' ward. I suggested that he was suffering from an overwhelming inferiority complex, and because of this he was constantly misjudging himself and exaggerating his faults. He was in fact a much more agreeable type than he would allow. As it turned out, the war ended while he was in the hospital, so that there was no question of his having to return to active service. Before he left hospital he had recovered his composure and his self-esteem. He felt that he could go out and face the world, and his parents.

There are many people like young Hartmann who alone just cannot come to terms with their problems, and help is needed in a search for a solution.

Symptomatic Depression

The stress of an adverse environment, if it is too great or lasts too long, can make a person ill with a depression. Unfavourable physical circumstances can do the same, and this is the second cause of depression that I wish to discuss. This basis for melancholia is far less common than reactive depression. The low mood can be the symptom of some disease, hence the name symptomatic depression. It can accompany any disease or injury to the brain. It is, for instance, very common in cases of the shaking palsy we call Parkinson's disease. It often follows a virus infection such as influenza, hepatitis or glandular fever, and the low spirits and sense of apathy can linger for months after recovery from the initial illness.

It can be brought on by poisoning with heavy metals like lead or mercury. Forty years ago there was quite a common infantile depression called pink disease. This was caused by mercury which was an ingredient of some teething powders, and once this item was banned the disease disappeared. Some drugs used to lower blood pressure can make the patient depressed, as can the contraceptive pill in some women who are sensitive to the contents.

Deficiencies in certain essential items of diet, especially members of the vitamin B group, can make the victim feel under the weather and miserable. Women have a much more sensitive and complex hormonal system than men. These substances regulate the menstrual periods, lactation after pregnancy, and so on. Imbalance of this system is common, and one of the symptoms of such an upset can be depression. Many women feel rather wretched and irritable just before a period, and some are unfortunate enough to have a real mini-depression each month, an experience they can find hard to endure. It is not unusual for women to date an episode of melancholia from the birth of a child. This illness reaches a peak of incidence at the menopause.

Addiction in any form can give rise to depression. The so called hard drugs like heroin, cocaine and the opiates are not a big problem in Britain, but there is evidence that many people are habituated to soft drugs like the barbiturates and Mandrax.

However, the greatest problem of all in Western society is, of course, alcoholism. Indeed, it must be one of the most common symptomatic causes of melancholia. It has been estimated that rather more than 1 per cent of the population over twenty years of age in England and Wales is an alcohol addict, and the figures for Scotland and Ireland are likely to be even higher.

Many of us enjoy a drink at a party and we are aware of how it acts as a kind of social lubricant. Some, who have on occasions taken too much, can appreciate the agony of that transient depression, the hangover. This is as nothing compared with the bitter remorse felt by the alcoholic who allows himself to think about his problem. He realizes to his disgust that he is in the grip of a habit which he is completely unable to drop, and yet he knows only too well that it is threatening his personality and his life style. Many alcoholics are acutely aware of this, but they resolutely refuse to admit it to another person. Without going into the clinical details of alcoholism, proof of its depressive nature is shown up by the very high figure for suicides among addicts. It is also a common cause of reactive depression among the partners of the victims.

Primary Endogenous Depression

This is the third, and in some ways the most interesting, type of melancholia. It is an illness in its own right, like shingles, a gastric ulcer, or gout. It has many different names such as plain endogenous depression, manic-depressive disease, psychotic depression, or simply melancholia. Names like this can be misleading as it is not every case that shows the extreme mood swings of the manic-depressive syndrome, and all the patients with the illness are not psychotic by any means. The term primary endogenous depression means that it is derived from internal sources, that it is a biochemical upset of brain function, and not in any way due to outside influences.

Mr Hall, a young up and coming business executive, illustrates well this type of depression. He came to see me because he was worried about holding down his job. He told me that he really enjoyed his work and until a few weeks before was confident that he was well on the way to carving out a successful career. However, in spite of his enthusiasm for his work, his ability to cope had been fading away, and he suggested that unless things improved, he could well lose his appointment at work. There was nothing to account for his disability in terms of adverse circumstances or any physical illness, and I diagnosed endogenous depression. I explained his problem by describing how there was some minor defect in his brain chemistry which could be corrected by way of drugs. Two weeks later he was more or less back to normal, and once more on top of his job. He told me his only worry was what would happen when he stopped the tablets! I told him that after two months of the treatment the dose would be reduced and then the drug would be stopped. By then his brain function would be back to a normal rhythm, and this is precisely what happened. After some three months of medication he was completely back to normal and independent of any drug.

This disease has been recognized by physicians ever since medicine was recorded in the Hippocratic clinics of classical Greece. Aretaeus, a doctor of Alexandria in the second century A.D., was the first person to note the mood swings of the illness, and to realize that mania, although very different from depression, was a part and parcel of the same disease.

Like the symptomatic group of the depressive disorders, primary endogenous depression is a comparatively rare condition, but for a number of reasons it is often missed, and this is a pity, as it is so easy to treat. Furthermore, scientists are learning a great deal from such cases about the basic mechanism of melancholia. Primary endogenous depression is brought about by an upset in the complex chemical processes in the brain. Some of these items are called neurotransmitters, as they assist in the passage of messages along the nerve fibres. If these substances are in short supply the patient feels depressed; if there is an excess he becomes elated.

Mania

I have already enumerated some of the symptoms of depression; the opposite reaction, that of mania needs to be described. As with melancholia there are degrees of mania. Minor conditions are called hypomania, and any person in this state is in splendid spirits, with an infectious type of gaity which can render the individual the life and soul of the party. Such people tend to talk too much, but the condition is compatible with a normal way of life.

Mr Jinks, a middle-aged man, had a minor depression following an attack of influenza. This low phase gave way to a state of mild elation. Before going off to work in the mornings, by rising at 5 a.m., he was able to start a room to room redecoration of his house. He bought a new car and was constantly in tearing spirits, so much so that his wife became worried about him and insisted that he saw the doctor.

When the latter asked her why she had made her husband come to the surgery she was somewhat embarrassed, but then admitted she felt he was going mad. With a chuckle of amusement her husband said he agreed with the suggestion, but added that he had found the experience most agreeable. The doctor explained the situation by saying that the man's motor was, as it were, over-revving, but it would probably settle down in a few days. They were advised that if in fact it got worse, the high moods could rapidly be controlled by drugs, and he congratulated them on being wise enough to consult him. After another week the elation did pass, and much to the wife's relief he returned to normal mood levels, but she had to admit she had never had so much help from her husband with the spring cleaning!

True mania on the other hand, is a shattering type of illness, even more disruptive than depression. The patient just cannot keep still or stop talking. He becomes angry or even violent if crossed, and is full of ideas that are blatantly phoney. One man told me he was going to make his fortune as he had invented an infallible scheme for laying bets, and even the inevitable failures in the system did nothing to deter him from the idea. The patient feels so well he cannot agree that his exuberance is in any way a disease. He spends far too lavishly, and at parties the wine flows like water. In the days before mania could be actively treated, the victim could die of sheer exhaustion.

Mrs Clark, the wife of a professional man, told me about her husband who was prone to both manic and depressive episodes. When he was down it was very distressing but she felt she was able to help and support him. With the greatest difficulty he was able to do his work, but she relieved him of every possible duty in the home. He was constantly in a state of utter exhaustion, and their social life was at an end. Such an existence was worrying and drab, but she just dreaded the time he would swing into mania. Once this had happened, he ceased to lean on her, or indeed listen to her, and she felt helpless to direct or assist in any way. There were now parties every night, and her husband, who drank far too much, could not stop talking, often embarrassing the company with his blue jokes. He became full of fanciful ideas, such as the adoption of children, or using the home as a refuge for prostitutes. It was an immense relief when his moods flattened out to normal, so that spending, talking and parties reverted to acceptable levels.

It is easy to see that mania is indeed the complete reverse of depression. The latter is a state in which confidence has wilted, thoughts and movements are painfully slow, and the future looks bleak and hopeless. In most cases of endogenous depression, there is no manic component, but if it does occur, there is no doubt about the diagnosis; the illness is due to a biochemical upset which can be changed by physical methods of treatment.

Endogenous depression has certain other features which make it different from other types of melancholia. The change of mood seems to come out of the blue for no apparent reason. The illness tends to run in families, and the victims are often the cream of our society, clever and hard working types. They are, in fact, very different from the unworthy creatures they feel themselves to be. Both sexes are afflicted in the same proportions, whereas with the reactive depressions there are two women sufferers for every man.

Recurrent episodes are common. The patient not only looks on the gloomy side of life, but her thinking can become irrational and she may even suffer from delusions of one sort or another. The disease is impervious to counselling, indeed talking may make the patient feel worse. A change of environment does not alter the mood, so that to suggest a long holiday in the sun away from home is a waste of time and money. The depressive phase always passes, but it may take months or even years to blow over. One of the features of this melancholia is that time seems to go very slowly, so that no matter how long it actually lasts, it appears to be interminable. I was interested in this condition long before there was any effective treatment available for the family physician to prescribe, and I found that the *average* duration was about eleven months. It was a long and wretched experience for the patient and her family. It was not easy for the general practitioner, who could only help his patients by giving them tablets to help them to sleep, and by constantly assuring them that the illness would eventually pass. I could reinforce this by telling the patient that I had seen recovery in such cases again and again, and I would keep on repeating that eventually their trials would in fact come to an end.

Today things are very different and the illness responds well to physical treatment, usually in the form of tablets. Those people liable to frequent recurrent episodes of either mania or depression can have these tiresome mood swings prevented by the continuous use of the simple salt, lithium carbonate. Most doctors will agree that the primary endogenous depression is the easiest form of melancholia to treat.

Secondary Endogenous-like Depression

The classification of depressive disorders is made more difficult by the fact that relatively mild reactive depressions can become severe, and they can then assume many of the features of endogenous depression. When this has happened, no matter what the basic cause of the condition is, the patient does not respond to counselling, but usually makes an excellent recovery with physical treatment.

Mrs Davidson was a middle-aged housewife. She looked after her home at the back of a shop and cared for her three children. Her husband ran the business. One night he had a coronary thrombosis and for months he was a cardiac invalid. Mrs Davidson rallied to the occasion, and with the help of a friend she ran the shop as well as attending to her other duties. She was obviously worried by what had happened, but she could cope.

After some nine months her husband had a second heart attack and died. The poor woman was literally paralysed with grief, and even before the funeral she had begun to have strange ideas. She started to insist that her husband was not dead, but had gone off with another woman. One could not reason with her, and she was so mentally disturbed she had to be admitted to a psychiatric hospital where she was given anti-depressant drugs. She came home a month later still on tablets. She had recovered and was indeed able to carry on with the difficult task of running her home, her family and the business. She certainly did not lack courage or ability. I called to see her six years later and found her behind the counter of the shop. She told me it was the work, and the support of her children that had kept her going, and she was keeping well.

The sudden disaster and its magnitude had forced this woman from a state of reactive depression into what I have called a kind of secondary endogenous depression. It had many features of a primary melancholia. She was deluded and unresponsive to counselling, but she made a rapid and sustained response to a simple form of physical treatment. This sort of syndrome is more common than the primary form which has no psychic trauma in the background.

The Spectrum of Depression

To sum up what I have been trying to say: depressive syndromes can be viewed as a kind of spectrum with normal sadness at one end of the scale, and severe psychosis at the other. At the mild extremity are the low moods we all experience and accept as a normal part of life.

Next comes the mild reactive depression, which is to some extent disabling. As it becomes more severe, the patient is less and less able to cope. The next phase is the secondary endogenous-like depression, and finally there is the severe primary form of melancholia.

Today the serious types are rare because the patient is spotted as being ill and receives treatment long before that stage is reached. The picture I have drawn is, of course, an over-simplification of a complex set of syndromes. It should be noted that unless the depression is brought on by some sudden violent trauma, all depressions start with mild, vague symptoms, so that all low-grade forms are not necessarily reactive. The primary endogenous depression, seen for the first time, can be misleading.

Amy Evans was a young woman of twenty-two who, just after the war, came to see me three months before her wedding. She had decided that she had made a big mistake, and that she was wrong in thinking of getting married. She was all for breaking off her engagement. At first she produced seemingly valid reasons for this attitude, and initially the problem seemed to be one of a reactive depression. However, with some psychotherapy and closer observation, it was shown to be an endogenous depression, the first in fact of many episodes which plagued her in later life. When the diagnosis was clear, she was given physical treatment and made a good recovery. The wedding took place as planned, and she has now been happily married for many years.

The majority of people learn to cope with normal sadness, but some pass into a state of reactive depression which can become so severe that the patient needs the help of a counsellor. A very small minority, like Mrs Davidson, sink under severe stress into psychosis and need physical treatment. Some people are overwhelmed by an unfortunate combination of circumstances. A woman of forty-five who loses her husband from some illness has to bear the stress of the bereavement, and this in turn may bring on an early and stormy menopause. In her distress she may become careless about her diet, and in this way her levels of the vitamin B complex become low. In spite of all these factors she may be able to carry on reasonably well, but an attack of influenza can become the last straw, and the lowering effect of the viral infection can initiate a severe depression.

Depression in one form or another is an extremely common condition in the community and in all parts of the world. I have defined what the doctor means by depression, and I have outlined the various types. People sometimes ask me, at what point in a depression should they seek advice. Quite rightly they suggest that it would be wrong to run to the doctor every time they feel a bit low and miserable, or suffer from a few sleepless nights. I would suggest that if the bad moods have lasted continuously for two weeks or more, then it is time to seek the advice of an expert. This could be the family doctor, but it might be a member of the Social Services or the Samaritans. Under some circumstances it might be the local vicar, or if it is a child who is ill, the school authorities. The important thing to bear in mind is that today, depression is a *treatable* illness, and advice of some sort must be obtained.

Chapter 2
The Patient's Attitude

At the start of the last chapter, I described Mrs Adams' reluctance to see a doctor. I put this first because this feature is such a common symptom of depression. Often the melancholic has a sense of injured bewilderment. It is a fearful experience, and many patients who have suffered from depression state firmly that no person who has not descended into this valley of despond can really appreciate just how the patient feels.

This is not altogether true. While many of these people are misjudged and misunderstood by relatives and even members of the caring professions, there are many psychiatrists and family doctors like myself who have never experienced a severe depression, but who nevertheless can understand the complete turmoil in which the patient finds herself. On the way home, Mrs Adams confided in her husband that, much to her surprise, she had realized that I really did seem to understand how she felt, and that I could describe some of her symptoms better than she was able to herself. The knowledge that someone else understands her can be a great boost to the low morale of the sick person; at last she feels she is not alone in her misery. One psychiatrist compared the situation of such a patient with that of a traveller in a foreign land who is lost with night coming on and a storm brewing. Suddenly she comes across a stranger who can speak her language and so is able to direct her back onto the right road.

Desolation

There are few people more misunderstood than melancholics. The gravity of the illness is underestimated, and the sheer agony of the experience is not appreciated by the majority of people. When the clouds of depression descend, all the pleasure goes out of life; everything becomes drab and colourless. Each little job is an effort, and a rather weird system of exaggeration comes into action. The patient tends all the time to make mountains out of molehills. If the child coughs, he is getting pneumonia; if the husband is late home from work he must have had an accident. Every time the telephone goes, it is someone with bad news. Letters go unopened for the same reason.

The ability to appreciate beauty also goes, and this defect creates a painful void. A doctor who worked in the English Lake District knew he was getting depressed when the magnificent views of the mountains lost their appeal to him, and this knowledge added to his depression. Powers of concentration go, so that distraction by way of reading or watching television are ineffective and hopeless. The good joke instead of provoking laughter gives rise to a sense of pain as once again the complete inability to enjoy life is underlined. The patient feels cut off from everyone as normal bonds of affection wilt, and this lonely wretchedness is made worse by the conviction that there is no hope; the victim is convinced she will never recover, and often she feels that in some way she is to blame for what has happened. To add to the misery, time drags, so that every minute seems like an hour. Melancholia really is the quintessence of desolation: *it is without doubt the most unpleasant experience known to man.*

Unworthiness

Feelings of unworthiness need some elaboration. In one form or another they are a common symptom. The idea may be general, in that the patient feels that she is the most fearful sinner ever born. She may feel that in some way she has let the side down, so that the family is breaking up and she is no longer worthy of her husband's affection.

On the other hand, the sense of blame may be attached to some specific action. One man was sure his troubles dated from when he had received a pound more change at the supermarket and had failed to declare this mistake at the till. Such peccadilloes can go right back in time. A patient once told me that he was being punished because some thirty years before he had stolen a valuable stamp from a school friend. To all but the patient this explanation of his depression was quite illogical. A Scottish woman who had been married for many years insisted on 'marrying' her husband again. After the war she had been married in a registry office. She was a Catholic, and in her state of depression she had decided that the illness was a punishment for her 'living in sin' with her husband, so she had a second marriage ceremony performed in church.

Only two things do not inevitably lose all value. Some melancholics find great comfort in music, and others derive considerable relief by talking to some sympathetic person about their troubles.

Causes of Depression

There are, of course, many ways in which the illness can start. It may be precipitated by some family calamity, as in the case of Mrs Davidson who suddenly lost her husband. The woman who is abandoned by her man can be even more upset, as in addition to losing her partner she has suffered an outright rejection and has been insulted in a particularly vicious way. If there is some traumatic event which has set the depression in motion, this is likely to be known to either the patient or her family. However, just occasionally, the patient is so fearful of the actual cause of her trouble, that she keeps the problem to herself. This not only makes it difficult for those who are trying to help her, but it is also bad for the patient. The bottling up of a worry is dangerous; there is some truth in the old saying that a trouble shared is a trouble halved.

Mrs Fletcher was a pretty young woman who was the only child of devoted parents. She married at twenty and moved ten miles away to a home of her own. There she became very tearful and depressed, and her new doctor could find no explanation for her trouble. She became so ill she was referred to a psychiatrist, who, finding no environmental basis for her trouble, tried her on anti-depressant drugs, but they did not help her in any way. About this time, one of my partners was called to see her mother who was in bed with lumbago. When he examined her, he found that she had a huge breast cancer which she had kept concealed for three years. The cause of Mrs Fletcher's depression was now obvious. She was in fact worried to death about her mother, as she knew about the lump.

When faced by serious trouble we can all of us become strangely illogical, and this is what happened to Mrs Fletcher. Her mother had resolutely refused to see a doctor about her trouble, and the younger woman did not feel that she could insist on her doing so. Like her parent, she was ambivalent about the problem; most of the time it scared her stiff, but there were occasions when she could persuade herself that it might not be cancer after all. If she did ask the doctor to call, the truth would be out. Not only would she have gone against her mother's wishes, but, by facing up to reality, she could have removed all hope and, as it were, handed her own mother her death warrant. This was a situation she could not tolerate, and so she evaded the issue and slumped into a depression.

When they marry, young people should pledge always to share, not only their worldly wealth, but also their worries. No nagging fear should ever be concealed from a spouse. Mrs Fletcher had every reason to be fearful for her mother, but in the vast majority of such situations the threat turns out to be far less dangerous than was anticipated. Our worst fears are only rarely confirmed.

Repression

Sometimes the trouble which afflicts us is so awful it cannot be contemplated at all, and so it is repressed in the subconscious mind. It can remain there, encysted as it were, without causing any major trouble until some external trauma resurrects the original situation and the troublesome active symptoms appear. This sequence of events is clearly illustrated by the following case history.

Miss du Toit was a well qualified and senior nursing sister. She was referred to me because she had developed a curious phobia. She was constantly afraid that she might poison someone. This was quite disastrous as regards her work in the wards. She found herself unable to give the patients their medicine, feeling that she had either administered the wrong drug or the correct medication in the wrong amount. When she went off duty she could not sleep for worrying in case she had done the wrong thing. To avoid these difficulties she applied for a transfer to non-nursing duties, and she was put in charge of the nurses' home. In no time she had fallen foul of the catering staff after visiting the kitchens and becoming suspicious of the food. Sometimes she ordered the destruction of a good meal just in case it poisoned her nurses. She was suspended from all duties and it was at this point that she came to see me.

She was completely at a loss to account for her actions, which she freely admitted were stupid and illogical, but she herself could do nothing to change her attitude. The basis for this phobia was uncovered by a process of long-term psychotherapy. In brief her story was as follows. The elder of two girls, she was jealous of both her sister and her mother. She was strongly fixated towards her father, whom she adored. She could recall getting into trouble for making her small sister eat some toadstools, but fortunately they were not poisonous. In childhood, the height of bliss was to sit on her father's knee. He had a good voice and her favourite song had the mawkish theme of a family in which the mother died leaving the father and daughter all in all to each other.

Her mother died of cancer when she was only thirty-six, but my patient had no recollection of any mourning reaction for her mother. Her response seemed to have been one of smug satisfaction. Miss du Toit never married; she told me that she had not met the man who could match up with her father. At thirty-six she developed a large pelvic lump, which she was convinced was a cancer like the one that had killed her mother at the same age. It turned out to be a benign fibroid tumour which was easily removed.

It was after this illness that she developed her phobia. After several sessions of counselling, the mechanism became clear. In her youth she had tried to poison her young sister, and she had wished her mother dead. These repressed thoughts caused no trouble until at thirty-six she felt she was 'condemned to the same fate as her mother', an appropriate punishment for all her evil thoughts. She was, in fact, reprieved, but the price was a dread of doing the same thing again, and hence her illogical fear of poisoning either her patients or fellow nurses.

Adverse circumstances are far and away the most common basis for depression. In general we learn to adjust, but if the calamity is too severe, or the stress goes on too long, the feelings of dejection interfere with the patient's thinking and upset her normal way of life. Someone has graphically described this process as circular waves of futile thought beating up against a pillar of fear. This unhappy state of affairs achieves nothing and is exhausting in the extreme. If anyone is quite unable to come to terms with a problem, help is needed. If this cannot be provided by parents, a spouse or some member of the family, then professional advice is necessary, and help by way of counselling should be sought.

Locating the Source of Stress

The individual who is aware of what is hurting her is in a sense fortunate; at least her 'enemy' is known and she can put the blame where it rightly belongs. Not everyone is as sensible and courageous as Mr Goadby. As a youth he was apprenticed to a firm of motor mechanics; he enjoyed the work and did extremely well. When his parents died, he was left a considerable sum of money and with this he set up his own business. The project was so successful he had to take on several mechanics, and go into partnership with a business manager. But the business world intimidated him, and from time to time he had a few weeks off work with a depressive illness. In the end he decided to sell the garage and resume work elsewhere as a master craftsman, and since then he has had no signs of any depression.

This man not only located the stress: he also found a solution to his problem. Compare his reaction with that of Mr Andrews. The last war came at just the right time for this young man. He was labouring in a granite quarry when hostilities started and he joined the marines. The new way of life suited him well. He was hard-working, enthusiastic and efficient, and he was rewarded with rapid promotion. Before the war had ended, he had acquired commissioned rank. When he returned to our village, he was welcomed back to the quarry where he was given a secure job and good pay, but it was a poor substitute for the glamour of service life. He married and had a family, and so felt more tied to his job than ever. He was promoted, but after the success and seemingly endless ladder of advancement in the marines, he felt he was a failure and should have done something better for himself and his family. Unlike Mr Goadby, he lacked the courage to break away from his unsatisfactory routine into some more ambitious project, and this feeling of failure was at least in part a basis for recurrent depressive episodes.

Miss Young was a parson's child, who at the age of seventeen became a lady companion to the daughter of an important county family. Her reward for her many years of service was in terms of status and travel, and to secure this she was content to accept a low personal salary. She had thoroughly enjoyed meeting interesting people, and being a valued retainer in a noble family. She had carried on with this work until her employer died at the age of sixty-four, and then Miss Young found herself out in the cold, having to stand on her own feet. She was awarded a generous pension, but inflation meant that it was decreasing in value year by year. Now an old lady, she found sheltered accommodation within her means, and furnished her room in a homely but elegant way. There were eight other residents of about the same age and social status as herself, but she was quite unable to make friends with them. They were bored to tears by her endless stories of the important people she had met, all referred to by their Christian names. The truth was that her only interest was living in the past. The present was dreary beyond words, and the future a frightening void. It was no surprise when she became very depressed. She lacked the drive to grow new roots or to find new friends, and she spent all her energy bolstering up her sagging morale by talking interminably about the good old days. It was much too painful for her to see that she was her own worst enemy.

Mrs Smythe came to see me with a multitude of complaints. She was an attractive woman of thirty-five, who had been married for ten years, but there were no children to the marriage. Quite early on she revealed that her husband was impotent, so that the chances of having the family she yearned for looked extremely bleak. The husband was willing to see me, and he too was as worried about the situation as his wife. He maintained that his wife suffered from long standing frigidity. The honeymoon period had been reasonably satisfactory, but after a few months of wedlock, he found he had been unable at any time 'to turn his wife on'. Over the years he had given up trying and lost interest, though he had no such problem with occasional encounters with other women. He was sure that his wife was becoming an alcoholic, and she admitted she had a drink problem. It was one way in which she could escape some of her frustrations. This unfortunate couple lived together, but they were sexually incompatible; incapable of loving or being loved.

These are some of the cases which find their way into the consulting room of the family doctor. Many have immense personal problems, and they have to find the courage to recognize factors which are the basis of their troubles. This is essential if they are to stand any chance of coming to terms with them. Understanding one's self and one's motivation can in itself be painful and demoralizing and a rather unpleasant revelation. Unfortunately, there is no magic wand in the form of a tranquillizer that is capable of changing our make-up, and no incantation that will make these problems disappear. These people need the help and understanding of experts, or groups versed in the handling of personal problems, and this type of case often means long-term therapy.

'Causeless' Endogenous Depression

On the other hand, patients suffering from the apparently causeless endogenous forms of depression are much easier to help, and I make no apologies for spending some time in discussing this subject, for the simple reason that primary endogenous depression is often missed by both the laity and professionals, simply because in the early stages of the illness, the condition may be heavily disguised. The patient herself may be completely unaware of what is going on, and the suggestion that she is suffering from a well-known and treatable physical type of illness may come as a pleasant surprise.

There is no mistaking the fully developed illness. If the

patient is so slowed down that she can hardly speak or move
the family rarely hesitate to seek expert advice and the
medical diagnosis is obvious. The same applies to the agitated
patient who cannot keep still and who paces the floor like a
caged animal, muttering to herself repetitive phrases such as,
'Oh dear, oh dear; this is awful, this is dreadful!' In the same
way, any layman realizes a person is ill if she becomes
blatantly deluded, as when the parson's wife, who for years
has been a dedicated 'unpaid curate' to the parish, claims she
is the most dreadful sinner ever born because she has
committed some unforgiveable sin.

Happily, today these gross manifestations are rare because
treatment is usually sought long before this stage is reached.
There is, however, one warning light which is all too often
ignored, and that is when the patient has hinted that she
wishes she was dead. There is a popular belief that the person
who threatens suicide will never actually take her own life, but
nothing could be further from the truth. Relatives are
especially likely to spot this threat to life, and once the danger
is suspected, medical help should be sought.

Difficulties in Diagnosis

The onset of primary endogenous depression is usually slow
and insidious and in the early stages of the illness the correct
diagnosis can be camouflaged. The most common error is to
view the problem as one of anxiety, and all of us are tricked
from time to time by this type of manifestation.

Mrs Innes came to see me about some sex problem. A
teacher at a grammar school, she was a highly intelligent
woman of thirty-two. I had spent several psychotherapeutic
sessions with her, and little progress was being made; and
then one morning she revealed how she hated waking up. She
said that always her first thought was that it would be quite
impossible to get through the day. This symptom was so
typical of endogenous depression that she was given anti-
depressant drugs and by the end of two weeks her problems
had started to fade away. What had initially seemed to be an
anxiety situation was in fact a problem of endogenous
depression.

Mrs Gibbs was a more typical case of this category and,

from the medical angle, easier to diagnose. There are many patients like her in the community. She was about forty when she came to see me and she disclosed she had a lump in her breast. I examined her with every care but I could find no evidence of any abnormality. When I tried to reassure her I sensed that she remained unconvinced, and when I asked her if she would like a second opinion she jumped at the idea. She was referred to a surgical expert, but he could find no organic trouble, and he was equally ineffective in his attempts to reassure the patient.

When I saw her again she was still very worried, and clearly convinced that she had a breast cancer. At first I tried to find out why she was so obsessed with the idea; and inquiries were made as to whether any relatives or friends had had this disease. This type of probing did no good. I spent a long time talking to her, trying to make her feel that I understood her problem, which was not an uncommon one to me. I told her I had helped many people like her in the past, and in the end I asked her if she would accept treatment by way of some tablets. She was clearly suspicious of this suggestion. She wanted to know what they were for and what they were supposed to do. I resorted to metaphor. I pointed out that if her television set was giving a distorted picture which was a pain and a grief to watch she did not throw the set away as if it had been irreparably damaged. She would call in an expert who by means of adjusting a few knobs at the back of the set, would restore a perfect picture.

I went on to suggest that while she thought she had clear-cut ideas as to what was wrong with her body, these were actually distortions and misinterpretations and that the drugs I was going to give her could effect a minor adjustment in her way of thinking, and so help her to sort things out. She was interested but did not altogether believe me, but I had won her husband over to my side and he promised to see that she followed the routine of taking the tablets.

Rather grudgingly, she finally agreed to a course of treatment to last for two weeks, after which the situation could be reviewed. I asked her to come and see me in three days, but if there were any problems to get in touch with me before then. She was on the telephone the next morning to say that her mouth was so dry she could hardly swallow. I assured her that this tiresome symptom was caused by the drug and that it would pass, and I reminded her that I had warned her that this would happen. When I saw her at the end of two weeks of treatment she was clearly improving. Rather sheepishly she admitted that she felt a lot better. When I asked her about the cancer, she said the worry had now gone because the tight feeling she had had across her chest had vanished. Before she left she posed the question, 'How can the taking of a few tablets make such a difference to the way one feels?'

I tried another metaphor. I explained that the drug had changed some minor fault in the way the emotional centres of her brain had been working, and this time I used the analogy of a clock that was running slow. The instrument was not broken; there was no serious fault, but the instrument was misleading and needed to be adjusted. She went on to make a complete recovery.

Fears of Madness

Sometimes the patient feels so tensed up and dreadful, she fears for her sanity. This idea is so appalling, she mentions it to no one, and then of course her worry intensifies. She has visions of being sent off to some psychiatric institution where she will end her days locked up, permanently divorced from her family. The doctor is the last person she wants to see as she is sure he will confirm her fears.

If I suspect the patient feels like this, I assure her that she is not going mad and that there is no chance that she will do so. I tell her that the mind is such a complex machine, wrong messages and misinterpretations are far more common than most people realize. I tell her of a personal experience. I was once driving my car along a country lane at dusk. As I rounded a corner, there was what I thought was a large owl standing in the middle of the road, and as I approached it rose into the air. I braked hard but it was too late, I hit it fair and square, and in my rear mirror I saw it lying on the road. Filled with regret, I stopped and went back to view the corpse, only to find it was a large black rag lying on the roadway. Had I not gone back to look, nothing would have convinced me that I had not hit some large bird. My eyes in the gathering darkness had completely deceived me. I suggested that the horrid feelings she was experiencing were also misinterpretations which could be reversed by taking suitable tablets.

Simulation of Physical Disease

Endogenous depression can closely simulate any physical disease you care to think about. I propose to give only one short example. Mr Jones came to see me with pains in his testicles. There was no gross evidence of any physical trouble, but he was both embarrassed and incapacitated. Finding no physical basis for his trouble, I referred him to a urogenital expert. The most searching investigations failed to show up the cause of his pain. The poor chap was utterly miserable, walking was difficult, and he had to sit down with the greatest care. He could not sleep at nights, and he was often in tears. Anglo-Saxon men do not as a rule weep in public, and this symptom alone was suggestive of depression. He was given full doses of anti-depressant tablets, and in quite a short time his pain had gone. Endogenous depression can appear disguised as some painful syndrome. In a survey of 600 cases of depression, I found pain in some form was a presenting symptom in 30 per cent of the cases. In most of these cases the discomfort was that of a headache, backache or pains in the muscles.

Schizophrenia

Schizophrenia is another form of mental illness. It, too, can be greatly relieved by modern drugs, but only twenty years ago it was virtually untreatable, and the psychiatric hospitals became overcrowded with such cases. It was such a serious disorder it was sometimes called the malignant disease of psychiatry, and just because it was such a dreadful affliction the very name, like the word cancer, still fills the average layman with horror.

In the past, melancholics whose depression simulated schizophrenia were often given a poor prognosis. This was unfortunate as the outlook in this type of case is very good. One patient of mine started with this syndrome well over forty years ago, and as a girl of seventeen she was taken from one specialist to another and given a uniformly bad prognosis.

How wrong all these consultants were. She is now an active and attractive woman in her early sixties.

The sort of thing that can happen is illustrated by the case history of Mr King. He was a married man of thirty with a family of four small children. He was a jobbing builder by trade and his life was a great success story. He had his own business, a lovely home, and trade was booming. He thought that he was happily married, but at a dance one weekend he was disconcerted to see his wife flirting with a neighbour. On the way home he told her how her behaviour had upset him. She was furiously angry and told him she was hurt to think that he had felt she was that kind of woman. He thereupon apologized for having taken the situation too seriously.

He continued to feel guilty about his allegations, and for the next few days bent over backwards to make amends with an extra show of affection. A week later he was completely bowled over when his wife told him bluntly that she was leaving him and the children to go off with the neighbour. He pleaded on behalf of their young children, but nothing he could say would make her change her mind. She left him to do the best he could with the family and the business. His elderly parents did their utmost to help by moving in to housekeep for him. His whole world seemed to have blown up in his face. He became so miserable and disturbed he was unable to carry on with his business. He became deluded and felt people were talking about him and sending messages through the wireless and television programmes.

He began to hear voices, and so strange was his behaviour he was persuaded to go to a psychiatric hospital for assessment and treatment. There he was given a blend of anti-psychotic drugs and improved. He was a highly intelligent chap and he decided that the facilities offered by the hospital gave him time to think and sort things out, well away from where everyone knew him and his troubles. He stayed for eight weeks, and when he did return home he was able to cope and run his business again. The clinical picture was one of schizophrenia, but in fact the breakdown was a reactive depression in which the trauma had been so severe that he had sunk into a secondary endogenous-like depression, which had responded well to treatment.

People suffering from chronic illness are by no means immune from depression. A jolly extrovert man with a long history of chronic bronchitis became complaining and miserable. He was sure his time was up, could not sleep at night, and was a real problem to himself and his wife. He was acting out of character with his normal well-balanced attitude to life. He was not a grouser by nature. He was given a course of anti-depressant drugs and after a couple of weeks he was his old cheerful self again. This type of melancholia can easily be missed in the aged. The old widow living alone, who starts to let things slide may well be depressed.

Mrs Lewis was an active widow of eighty-four who had never had any serious illness in her life. She lived alone, well supported by her family. She enjoyed doing the daily chores, visiting the young people, and playing bridge with her elderly neighbours. Suddenly she was overwhelmed by a state of complete exhaustion. She felt that she had been struck down by some serious bodily illness. Her family blamed her age and decided she was now too old to cope on her own. The daughters took her to live with them for a while. In fact there was nothing physically wrong, and she was given the appropriate drug treatment for depression. Within a month she was well enough to go home, run her house again, and once more settled to regular games of bridge. No old person should be allowed to die of so called senility without having a trial course of anti-depressant drugs. With this routine some of these people make a dramatic recovery.

Disguised Depression
There are a few people with endogenous depression who never quite reach the stage of feeling low in any way, so that it is possible to have the paradoxical situation of a patient suffering from melancholia who does not feel depressed. The illness expresses itself as patches of intermittent anxiety, and the patient never sinks as low as the depressive threshold.

Mrs Hardy was such a patient and with her it took me a number of years to reach the correct diagnosis. She was as a rule a vigorous hard working woman, but every so often she would come along with some ache or pain which sounded very much like an organic syndrome. The story was such that she usually needed to have a second opinion. She saw a surgeon for abdominal pain; a gynaecologist for pelvic symptoms with heavy periods; a throat specialist when she had great difficulty in swallowing, and an orthopaedic man for her bad back. Nothing definite was ever found; the symptoms were always different, and after a few weeks they always cleared. The patient remained fit and well until the next episode which occurred after a year or two of good health. When it dawned on me that these attacks could be depressions in disguise, I discussed the matter with her. I found that each illness was followed by a period of elation which she much enjoyed. She had boundless energy and could work until all hours. She found it hard to sit down. When her husband once begged her to relax and take it easy, she replied cheerfully, 'You might as well ask a child with measles to wipe away her spots.'

Clearly, she was prone to pleasurable attacks of hypomania, of which I had been unaware, but this story confirmed my idea that her illnesses were indeed episodes of camouflaged depression. After that, once a genuine organic illness had been excluded, she was given appropriate treatment and was soon back to normal. She became able to recognize what was happening herself, and when she felt ill she asked for another course of tablets rather than a consultation with some specialist.

Changes in Behaviour Patterns

There is one other final disguise for this illness which can happen at any age; and this is a sudden change in the behaviour pattern of the patient which is quite out of keeping with her normal way of life. The usually sober person takes to drink; the honest housewife is caught shoplifting; the church warden who is a J.P. and a pillar of society is caught exposing himself to children. By no means all shoplifters and exhibitionists are depressed, but a few are, and because of an illness the splendid reputation of a lifetime can be ruined.

A housewife came to see me because she was very worried about her husband. He had taken to gambling and was frittering away his savings. He had never done this in his life before. He was persuaded to see me and I found he had all the symptoms of depression, and when given anti-depressant drugs he lost all the urge to gamble. There is no such simple remedy for the addicted gambler, but this man's bad habit was a symptom of his depression.

Symptomatic depression was mentioned in the last chapter, and it is obvious that with any melancholic syndrome it is important to identify any physical illness which could be the basis of the low moods. The man who is feeling wretched because of latent pernicious anaemia needs regular injections of vitamin B12, and these will rapidly improve the quality of life for him. The young woman on the contraceptive pill may feel a great deal better without it and must adopt some other form of birth control. The patient who has been pitched into melancholia from an attack of influenza, or some catastrophe like a stroke, may well improve on a course of anti-depressant drugs.

Endogenous depression is certainly the easiest form of melancholia to treat, and from the case histories I have given I have shown how with a combination of drugs and supportive measures a rapid recovery can be effected. However, this kind of depression is not the most common of the depressive syndromes and I would hate to give the impression that all the victims of black moods can find the solution to their problems in a box of tablets. The most common form of melancholia is the reactive type; that is, the person who is weighed down by misfortunes in his environment, or in his own character. These people cannot be made well with drug therapy and, as I have already pointed out, they need the help of some counsellor. Psychotherapy and counselling are important forms of treatment that will be described in detail later. Many problems which at one time seem insuperable can be solved with expert help; life becomes more meaningful and pleasant, and the person who once felt defeated and unutterably feeble derives the greatest satisfaction from rising above her difficult circumstances. It is indeed possible, in one way or another, to defeat depression.

Chapter 3
The Family's Reactions

Amongst people in general, and unfortunately this includes some members of the caring professions, there are two kinds of illness; the respectable and the not-so-respectable, and most forms of nervous breakdown come into the second category. This attitude is quite illogical and wrong, but there is no denying that it exists in all levels of society.

A patient of mine applied to enter the police force. He had all the background qualifications but he had to be interviewed by a senior officer before the final decision was made. All questions were answered satisfactorily and then with a chuckle his examiner told him there were two final, rather silly queries. The first was had he ever had venereal disease? He cleared this hurdle. The second was had he ever seen a psychiatrist? When he admitted he had done so, he was promptly failed; he was not even asked why he had needed such an opinion.

Crippling joint diseases, heart attacks and cancer are considered to be honourable wounds in the battle of life, entitling the victim to every sympathy. Nervous complaints are different. Acute grief is allowable provided the process does not go on too long. Friends and neighbours rush in to help and sympathize until the funeral is over, but they often find it difficult to sustain their efforts over a long period. People tend to find that the bereaved partner is difficult to fit into parties, and so is often left out of social gatherings and quietly forgotten. The tendency is that if the widow is coping well she is ignored, but if over the weeks she is not able to master her grief she is looked on as an embarrassment to her friends who tend to become more and more unsympathetic and critical.

Apart from this state of mourning, depression and anxiety from other causes are looked on as rather disreputable affairs. Like the senior police examiner, the public are inclined to feel that psychiatric problems are as discreditable as venereal disease, although any thinking person knows they are very different. People suffering from a nervous breakdown are mentioned as little as possible in polite society, and if they are talked about, euphemisms are employed to belittle the problem. The sick person is said to have become strange, difficult or eccentric, or has just let himself go. Any term which could imply a psychiatric illness tends to be feared. Because of their danger to society, the victims of venereal disease are offered expensive treatment under the veil of complete secrecy. The attitude of the medical profession as a whole is very different towards the anxious or depressed patient.

In most places the psychiatric casualty has a low priority status. Just as the public view the person who is suffering from her nerves as someone who tends to imagine things and wilfully wallows in her grief so the psychiatric patient tends to be pushed to the back of the queue. If she tries to make an appointment to see her family doctor she is likely to be asked embarrassing questions by the receptionist and the chances are that she will have to wait several days for an appointment.

Alienation From the Family
I have gone to some length explaining how often the psychiatric patient is misunderstood because unless friends and relatives have experienced this type of illness themselves they tend to share the popular attitude. The husband who would be kindness itself to his wife if she had fallen and broken an arm can be quite a different person when faced by a tearful wife who has no honourable wounds to show. His attitude is painfully ambivalent. He loves his wife, but he hates her moods; he feels baffled, thoroughly irritated and on the

defensive. The most usual reaction is to assume the tough bullying attitude of advising her to pull herself together and to behave in the robust manner he is able to maintain.

On the other hand, he may try to ignore her problem, going out as much as possible, working overtime at the office, and in general withholding the support he should be giving her. Most psychiatric illnesses are slow and insidious in their onset and relatives are both mystified and worried by the changes they can see taking place and at a loss to know what to do about it. If a medical opinion is suggested, this is often firmly refused and the family do nothing but just hope the whole horrid episode will soon go away.

One of the reasons why a nervous breakdown is so disconcerting and upsetting and more difficult to manage than physical illness is that the normal lines of communication between the patient and the family have broken down. They cannot discuss problems in a rational manner. It is as if a thick piece of plate glass had been lowered between the patient and those who are close to her.

In a small minority of cases, the onset of the illness is sudden, and then the relatives are liable to panic and they rush to seek medical advice. Old people living alone sometimes live on diets which are grossly defective in vitamins, but if such a person contracts some infection like pneumonia, an acute confusional state can be precipitated. The family feel well able to cope with the chest infection, but once the old person starts some irrational chatter and begins to see things they are sure the old lady is going mad, and they are frightened and upset. Happily, the mental breakdown that begins suddenly like this is usually one of the easiest to treat. Often the vivid hallucinations soon disappear, as in the case described above, if large doses of Vitamin B are given. Mania is more likely to be of sudden onset than depression, but whatever the cause, it is a great consolation to relatives to know that the outlook in such cases is very good.

Plain Dealing

If it is felt that the patient should see a doctor or a psychiatrist, trickery or deception must never be used. If ever I heard of a patient needing help who would not come to my rooms to see me I was always prepared to visit her at home, but I always insisted that the patient was told beforehand of the arrangement. Sometimes the relatives would suggest that I called in casually for a social cup of tea, but deceit of this kind is not permissible. If it was felt that the patient was so disturbed that she might run away if she knew that I was going to call, then I would give the relatives a precise time for my visit, and the patient could then be told that I was coming at the husband's invitation when the family actually saw the car at the door. In this way I have met some very indignant and angry patients, but I never had a case who harboured any lasting resentment. An honest approach may provoke transient anger, whereas deceit rankles indefinitely.

The same kind of thing applies to a consultation with a psychiatrist. The patient must be told in advance, and there must be no nonsense like calling him a neurologist, or a friend of the family doctor; he must be called a psychiatrist. If this causes embarrassment, it must be left to the consultant or the general practitioner to explain the move. Confronted by the situation, the patient usually accepts it and finds the medical advisers more understanding and helpful than she anticipated.

First Attacks
The first attack of depression can be very misleading and hard to understand. The patient is at a loss to explain what is going on, the relatives are both worried and mystified, and even the family doctor may not spot the correct diagnosis in his initial contact with the patient. Take, for example, the first attack of primary endogenous depression in a girl of seventeen who was sitting important school examinations. She was a clever girl who had always done well at school and her parents were inordinately proud of her achievements.

A few weeks before her examination she started becoming very worried, could not sleep at nights, and she was quite certain she was going to fail. Sympathetic at first, the parents assured her that the ordeal would soon be over, but when these tactics failed, they became extremely anxious. They went to see the headmaster who was most understanding and helpful. The second mistress was called in, and the teachers assured the troubled parents that they had nothing to worry about and that the girl was assured of a good pass.

Armed with this good news, and feeling somewhat irritated that their daughter was giving them such a burden of worry, they tried new tactics. Firmly they told her she was stupid to be so upset, implying her attitude was all an act. Fortunately for all concerned, the depressive mood did pass before the examination took place. The girl did very well, and both teachers and parents wisely nodded their heads as if to say, 'I told you so'. However, her low moods were not just due to examination fears. This was in fact the first of many episodes of depression which went on to torment her through her life.

I saw her in her second attack. The diagnosis was then obvious and she responded very well to treatment. She told me about the first episode of illness which she recognized as being similar to the second. One can hardly blame the parents for adopting the attitude they did. The point at issue is that both they and the teachers had completely failed to see that the girl was actually ill.

Betty Bains was a competent shorthand-typist who at twenty-four had an excellent job in a local firm. She was very attached to her aged grandmother, and soon after the old lady died from a coronary thrombosis Betty herself developed a fear of heart disease. Her mother brought her along to see me, and a physical examination showed no evidence of any organic trouble, but she was obviously very worried. I spent some time alone with her, reassuring her, and listening to what she had to say about her grandmother. Even before they left, while I felt that the mother had gratefully accepted the medical verdict, I knew the younger woman had remained unconvinced by what I had said.

She had an appointment to see me again, but before that date I was called to see her at her home. After struggling to work for a couple of days, she had taken to her bed, saying she was far too weak and ill to get up. While I did not retract my views on her heart, it was clear that she was a very sick woman. She was sleeping badly, and for some time had been constantly in tears. When she was questioned, she admitted that she felt there was no future for her; she was indeed quite a different person from what she had been three months before.

A secondary endogenous-like depression was diagnosed and with appropriate treatment she made a good recovery.

In this case the parents were more shaken by the experience than the patient. The latter was only too pleased to be back to normal. The father remembered how his sister and one of his uncles had suffered from a similar type of illness and one of them had spent some time in a mental hospital. When husband and wife had discussed the problem, they reluctantly decided that their girl had inherited the family taint. The fact that the patient's great-uncle was a university professor and her aunt the head mistress of a big school was no consolation. The young woman actually did very well in her career. She was liable to recurrent attacks of depression, but these were easily controlled. But her parents told me that, no matter what her symptoms were, their first thought was that this was another attack of her nerves, and their hearts went into their boots with a mixture of shame and apprehension.

Fear of Mental Illness

This attitude was quite understandable fifty years ago when nothing active could be done to help the melancholic patient. However, in spite of the excellent outlook with treatment, fear lingers in the hearts of patients and their families alike. The bogey of depression as a menacing mental illness is still with us today. Like Betty's parents, many people worry about the hereditary factor. They ask themselves, will the children suffer from similar troubles, and will the illness in a parent have a bad effect on growing children? The ordinary reactive depression which is so very common that almost every family must at some time have experienced it, is not hereditary. However, the primary endogenous illness does seem to run in families. It may be some consolation to realize that on the whole these people are a highly intelligent group. In his autobiography, Julian Huxley[1] described how he and his extended family suffered from this affliction. Winston Churchill referred to it as his black dog. The melancholic is in good company. Before there was any active treatment to cut the illness short, this kind of worry was thoroughly justifiable, but the consequences of a controlled depression are very much less drastic.

Effect on Children

The question as to whether or not periods of melancholia have an adverse effect on young children is another matter. Illness of all kinds causes some disruption of family life, but an occasional episode, as when one or other of the parents goes down with influenza, is just a part of normal life, and is generally accepted as such by the children. Indeed a break in routine can be a welcome interlude. As regards depressive illnesses, my feeling is that children are tolerant of what is going on, especially if the trouble does not last too long, and I feel that manic-depressive parents are less of a problem to the children than the chronically anxious parent who can be constantly fussing and over-protective. The mother's illness is certainly worse for a small family than one in the father. Long ago, I remember an eminent psychiatrist saying that she would have no objection to one of her daughters marrying a person liable to depressions, although she would do her best to discourage a liaison with a schizophrenic. This to my mind is a very sensible way of looking at the problem.

The Role of the Family

The relative who is surprised and baffled by the first episode of a depressive illness deserves every sympathy, and can hardly be blamed if the wrong things are said and the patient is offered bad advice. However, with subsequent attacks, he should be on his guard, and have a better idea what to do. I have always felt that the crowning success of treatment was when the patient herself was prepared to come along and see me if ever she felt the clouds of depression descending again. While this occasionally did happen, it was only a small proportion of recovered melancholics who did so. Far more commonly the patient with insight would say to herself when she felt she was slipping, 'This time I will get over it myself; this time I will show them all that I can master the situation.'

Because of this I found that alerting the next of kin was a far more reliable safeguard and before discharging the patient from my care I used to make a point of talking to the couple together about the situation. I would tell the convalescent that there was a good chance that the trouble would never recur; but if that did happen, the sooner he or she reported sick the better. Once again, I would suggest that continuous low moods that last for two weeks are a clear indication for a medical opinion. I would tell the husband that if his wife did not feel like making the effort, he should bring her along, or at least come and see me himself so that we could discuss the matter together. In the euphoria of the recovered state, the wife can usually accept this advice given to her husband, and she has no objection to a discussion of her illness. She tends to belittle it, and is likely to say that it just will not happen again.

Warning Signs

Relatives who have once become alerted to the trouble, can be very skilled at spotting the onset of a depression. The patient's voice can become flat and expressionless, and this is particularly noticeable over the telephone. She tends to sigh constantly, becomes forgetful, and lets things slide in a way she would never normally do. Cooking becomes repetitive, and not as well executed as it is when she is well. She becomes scratchy and irritable for no real reason, and is often sexually unresponsive. There is invariably some sleep disturbance, and the spouse may be more aware of this than the patient. One woman claimed to sleep well, but her husband told me that she was so restless in the night that more than once he had had to abandon his side of the bed and climb in again on the other side. The eyes lose their lustre and expression. The patient may seem to have lost the ability to smile, or occasionally assumes the rather wooden smirk of the smiling depression, which can deceive the unwary, especially if she denies feeling depressed. Strange habits may be the prodrome to another episode. This may be a constant clearing of the throat, or playing with the mouth, as if the dentures were uncomfortable. Whenever the next of kin sees such a red light, some action should be taken.

Quite as important as spotting the depression, is the relatives' knack of appreciating that the patient is a suicidal risk. There is a very small minority of patients who are so frightened of such feelings that they seek the help of a physician, but they are rare birds. As with depression itself, it is usually the relatives who are the first to realize what is happening, and the wise ones let the doctor know.

Mrs Sharp was such a person. I was looking after her husband, who had lost his father from a coronary thrombosis, and he appeared to be worried about his own heart. I could find no evidence of any trouble in his chest and I felt that his anxiety was attached to the mourning reaction over his parent. I started him on a course of psychotherapy. One evening surgery Mrs Sharp rang me up, and told me she was extremely bothered about her husband. She went on to say that before she was married she had worked as confidential private secretary to some business man. This man had killed himself, and she felt that her husband had similar symptoms. I asked her to bring him along to see me that same evening, as soon as he was back from work. She did so, and I found that he was indeed far more depressed than I had realized and that he had harboured ideas of suicide. These were discussed with him.

The patient with these fearful thoughts is helped by discussing them with an expert, in much the same way as the discussion of any really intimate problem often gives some immediate relief. I told him I realized how bad he must have felt and that I was going to start him on some medical treatment. After a few weeks on anti-depressant drugs the danger had passed and he went on to make a full recovery. This case was very similar to that of Betty Bains who grieved over the loss of her grandmother. Sometimes physical treatment by way of drugs is far more effective than any form of counselling.

If this danger of suicide is suspected by relatives, then it is imperative that medical advice be sought as a matter of urgency. In the depressed patient, the wish to be dead is no transient fancy but a real threat to life that can rapidly be relieved by expert treatment. It is mainly due to the better diagnosis and treatment of depression that the average suicide rate over the past decade has fallen drastically in Britain. If the patient cannot be persuaded to visit the surgery, most doctors with an interest in this subject are prepared to make a home visit and, as we have already seen, the sympathetic handling of the case by a doctor can offer great relief to the patient, no matter how apprehensive she was before the interview.

Vigilance During Treatment

Another duty of the spouse of a melancholic, is to see that the patient follows the advice that has been given. This means seeing that the tablets or the medicine are taken on time as directed. If there are unpleasant side effects, the patient must be encouraged to bear with them, or if they appear to be too severe, he should then contact the doctor and discuss the matter with him, but no change in the routine should be made until the physician has been consulted and has issued fresh advice on the matter. The husband must see to it that his wife follows a daily routine that is within her capacity. Generally speaking, with depression, lying in bed all day is not a good idea. The patient must be encouraged to accept a reasonable state of activity, and along with this she must eat proper meals.

Simple physical activities are usually more acceptable than brain work, so that cleaning the brasses is better than tackling a crossword puzzle or attempting to read a book. The patient needs to be tactfully coaxed along, and this is no easy task. She is likely to be both irritable and tearful, and may well question the propriety of any suggestion. If she is deluded in any way, she may keep on repeating her irrational fears or suggestions. Anger, or a flat contradiction of such ideas, does no good, and only tends to make the patient feel more cut off than ever from the family. It is always better to blame the illness rather than the person, and a response to phoney ideas should be countered in words to this effect. 'This is the way you feel because of your illness. It must make you feel quite dreadful, but these horrid feelings will pass, and you will be well again.'

A hearty, jolly attitude is usually not acceptable, being out of context with the patient's feelings. A joke is painful rather than funny. The glum silence of the patient can often be painful for the husband who is doing all he can to help in very difficult circumstances. All his extra work and effort to keep things going, seem to be unappreciated. The melancholic is unable to think nice things, and finds it almost impossible to say them; but when the illness is over she often expresses her gratitude for the patience and understanding of all concerned.

Talking

There are some patients who get considerable relief from talking. Their conversation is self-centred, and repetitive, and can go on like a scratched gramophone record. It can be extremely hard on the person who has to listen to the out-pourings which can quite literally go on for hour after hour. As one patient put it later, when he had recovered, talking itself had been a great help to him and, at that particular point in his illness, had been his only source of relief. The spouse may well have friends who are prepared to lend a helping hand in this exercise. Much of the time one just has to listen and, wherever possible, make noises of approval or understanding.

Open confrontation should be avoided, as the patient is rarely helped by a flat contradiction. On the other hand, to agree with some wrong idea or a delusion only causes it to become more entrenched. Where possible agree, but counteract false ideas by suggesting that it is the illness which makes the patient feel that way. While an understanding physician is prepared to listen to the patient's troubles, it is quite impossible for him to be a recipient of this kind of outpouring for more than a very limited time. One thing to be borne in mind is that if the patient is under active treatment this phase of talking too much will pass, but it is a mistake to think that if she is given her head she will be able to talk herself out of her troubles. This is most unlikely to happen.

Regression

It is well known that when a person becomes ill, from any cause, there is an element of regression: the invalid goes back to childhood and becomes dependent on others, just as once she was dependent on parents. This is a normal situation in any illness and patients like children can be helped by distractions and surprises.

A huge West Indian husband of one of my patients came to see me to discuss some of his wife's problems. I told him that I appreciated that he must have considerable difficulties at times because of his wife's strange moods. He assured me confidently that he knew how to manage her. I looked at his broad leather belt, and wondered if that was what he used.

How wrong I was! When I asked him outright what he did in such circumstances he replied, 'Ah jes burst into tears.' I felt sure that this manoeuvre must have surprised his small wife and done her a great deal of good. No matter how kind one is at the low point of a depression, the relatives' best endeavours may appear to make no difference, but once the patient has recovered she will often say how much ideas which had appeared to be scorned at the time did in fact help.

Deferring Decisions

I have mentioned that at times the patient can have quite false ideas as to what has caused her troubles. She may blame the house, her husband's job, or her daughter's fiancé. She may demand that the situation be changed, saying that if she cannot have a new home in some other area she will simply leave the family to cope as best they can. One of the basic rules in the management of a depressed patient, therefore, is to take no far-reaching decisions until the patient has been given a full course of treatment. Once recovery has set in, the correct decision is much more likely to be made.

Amy Evans had been all in favour of handing her ring back to her fiancé. She was dissuaded from doing so, and after her recovery she was more than a little grateful for having received such advice and she went on to make a very successful marriage.

A farmer came to live in our village and after a few months he decided he had made a big mistake and was all for returning to the area from which he had come. This change-over would have cost him a great deal of money. When I saw him he was obviously depressed and he was urged to have some active treatment before coming to a final decision. He did this, and twenty-five years later he was still farming contentedly in our community.

If, after recovery, the patient feels the same about her problem, then her ideas are worthy of serious consideration. A woman of seventy came to live close to her daughter in her retirement. This meant a move of only twenty miles from her own village. She became very miserable and depressed, and when I saw her she told me she knew why she felt so low; she was missing her friends and the place in which she had lived all her life. A prolonged discussion of her problem was no help to her but she improved on anti-depressent tablets and started to put down roots in the new environment. She was a woman of character and had no wish to take tablets for ever and she asked if she could stop them. When she did so she became depressed again, so they were resumed. She improved again, but decided that the only sensible thing to do was to go back to her own village. As it happened, she was allocated a small flat, and she has lived there now for some five years enjoying good health, without the need for any more tablets. The point I am trying to make is so important, I feel it is worth repetition. *The melancholic should never be allowed to make far reaching decisions in a state of depression.* The relatives must steel themselves to resist this type of suggestion and if they need help their doctor will certainly reinforce their ideas in this matter.

The Danger of Partial Recovery

Another duty of relatives is to see that when the patient is under treatment, her recovery is indeed complete. After the horror of a depression, the patient is so grateful for any relief given, she may well be content to carry on in what is called an arrested state of depression. Only 80 per cent well, she feels it would be churlish to complain when she feels so much better than she did when her melancholia was at its worst. It is not everyone who has the character and good sense of one of my patients. When she came to collect a new prescription she told me that while she had to admit she was very much better she was still not herself and she did not fancy living the rest of her life 20 per cent under par. Her treatment was changed and soon she was completely well, and has remained so for the past twenty years. If she herself had not pointed out the defect I would not have known about it.

The recovered patient may be reluctant to complain after the doctor has done so much, or she may be tired of visiting the psychiatric clinic. She tells everyone she is quite well when recovery is only partial. The next of kin who knows the norm of the sick person is in an ideal position to estimate a complete recovery, and if they feel there is indeed room for improvement, they should say so. It is often easier for them to state the problem than the patient.

Mr Gilliver had been in and out of mental hospitals for some sixteen years. He was an obsessional hardworking type and held down a responsible job, but life was difficult for him as he had never made a complete recovery from his illness. When the new drugs for depression came along, I tried them on him and after a few weeks a full recovery was achieved. When he came to collect a new prescription he told me that he felt better than he had done for many years. At last he was back to normal. His wife made a point of coming to see me to tell me how much better he was. After some sixteen years of arrested depression he was back to full health. Partial recovery is not good enough, and this should be pointed out to the doctor by the relatives if they are not happy about the patient. It is not easy for the doctor sitting in the surgery to know the full situation, and many patients are only too ready to put on a good face.

The treatment of depression, whether by counselling or physical measures, is not easy for the patient, and they need the support and encouragement of relatives to seek help in the first place, and to carry on with the treatment once this has been initiated. Depression is not only an individual's illness: it is a problem for the whole family.

Note

[1] Julian Huxley, *Memories*. Penguin, 1970.

Chapter 4
Where To Turn For Help

Having worked most of my professional lifetime as a family
doctor, I feel that the general practitioner is the obvious first
choice for an adviser in the problem of depression. I am well
aware that while most melancholics are prepared to take this
step, there are some who are reluctant to do so, and one of the
reasons for this is the way emotional disorders were dealt with
in the past. Not every physician has the same experience in
handling depressives that I have and until recently the mild or
moderate cases of the depressive syndrome went largely
unrecognized. Here is a letter written to a consultant by a very
competent family doctor some forty years ago.

> I have been attending this patient for about two months on this
> occasion. He complains of sleeplessness, loss of appetite, tiredness
> etc. He has been attended by me before on many occasions for
> similar complaints. I can find no physical signs to account for it.
> Urine – no sugar or albumen. I have treated him as a neurosis,
> but he does not improve. Perhaps you would be good enough to
> see him.

The symptoms listed, and the fact that the man had
suffered from recurrent episodes of a similar illness would
ensure the diagnosis of primary endogenous depression today;
but in 1939 little was known about the early symptoms of this
illness. Even twenty years ago, the general practitioner had

little to offer by way of practical help in many of the cases he came across at his surgery. Outside the dread portals of the old style mental hospital there was little chance of active treatment: there were certainly no drugs to effect a rapid recovery. Just because the illness was in many ways untreatable, medical practitioners did tend to fight shy of the issue, and as far as possible avoid such cases. Unfortunately, with some doctors this tradition has persisted.

However, in general things are very different today. Modern medical students are well trained in these matters; they know what to expect, and what to do. When I was a medical student fifty years ago, the training in psychiatry was abysmally inadequate and when I qualified I was so ignorant in the subject that I too tended whenever possible to avoid such cases. Today psychiatry, which is a study of emotional disorders, is one of the five major subjects in the final examination which all students have to pass. Much more attention is being paid to this important branch of medicine. Only last year, a leader in one of the prominent medical journals stated that the improved outlook in depressive disorders was in part a direct consequence of better techniques employed by general practitioners. The victim of a long-standing emotional problem wrote a paper in the *British Medical Journal* which had this to say about his family doctor: 'I am blessed in having a friendly G.P. who is prepared to listen sympathetically to my problems, do everything he can, speak the correct kind words.' He went on to say that one G.P. like this was worth an infinite number of social workers, and much much more than the 'oh-so-objective registrars'. (The latter were trainee psychiatrists.) Obviously this man found the support and help he needed in his family doctor; and this is the way it should be, but we do not live in an ideal world, and this happy relationship is not always forthcoming.

The G.P.'s Advantages

No matter who is treating the depressed person, the first step is to look for the basic cause of the trouble; and here in many ways the family doctor is in an advantageous position. I have already pointed out that the majority of depressions are reactive, that is, they are due to adverse circumstances, and the general practitioner should be able to deal with many of these cases. If, however, there is no environmental factor, then the patient must be given a complete medical examination to exclude organic disease as a cause of the trouble, and the family physician can do this without any delay. The symptoms may spring from such things as anaemia, diabetes, a thyroid upset, and a whole host of other illnesses. It may come from some drug the patient is already taking, which will be named in the medical records. The doctor may also realize that the patient is a member of a family prone to manic-depressive illness.

Another big advantage is that he is free to treat his patient in any way he thinks fit. He may use psychotherapy, or he may feel that some psychotropic drug is the best remedy, and these he can prescribe. He can, if he likes, combine the two types of treatment. One of the disadvantages of psychotherapy is that the process is very time consuming, and it is not every family doctor who is prepared to adopt these measures. Some are extremely skilled in the art of dealing with people who are in trouble, and even in quite short interviews they get excellent results. Many of these practitioners would reject the term psychotherapy as being too pretentious for their mode of treatment, and yet the key to their success is the clever way in which they handle the emotional side of the problem.

To me, psychotherapy is when the patient is given the chance of unburdening herself of her troubles, which are often intimate or embarrassing, to some expert she knows and trusts in an atmosphere of complete confidence. Secrets may be revealed which are as sacred as those heard in the confessional. There is no need to employ a Freudian couch to effect such measures, and every case does not take up an eternity of time.

To sum up what I have been trying to say: some doctors are naturals at putting the patient at ease, and, in a minimum of time, they can persuade the patient to divest herself of her worries, and with a little reassurance she begins to feel a great deal better. Some of us feel compelled to take more time over the process, and I am afraid that there are others who are so upset and embarrassed when the patient starts to unburden herself that they are of little use.

The Role of the Psychiatrist

There are cases of depression which for one reason or another require the expert help of the psychiatrist. This may be because there are diagnostic difficulties, or because the patient is extremely disturbed and is in need of treatment beyond the scope of the family doctor. At the beginning of the nineteenth century, before there was any anaesthesia, the most feared figure in the medical world must have been the surgeon. Operating on a fully conscious patient was a grim and ghastly procedure, and it was the sight of such an operation that finally put Charles Darwin off medicine as a career.

This mantle of fear and distrust has now fallen onto the shoulders of the psychiatrist. Such a reputation is quite unwarranted, but it is very prevalent on this side of the Atlantic. In the United States those who can afford his fees use the psychiatrist much as a practising Catholic consults a priest. For any problem in life, certainly when there is some emotional upset, the psychiatrist is consulted.

If the Americans use him too much, the British tend to under-employ him. He is certainly not the bogey-man as envisaged by many sick people. When I was working in a psychiatric hospital I came across this attitude; the patients often entered my consulting room tense with fear. After the first interview, many told me how relieved they felt to find that they could talk to me, to discover that I was quite human. They had dreaded the face-to-face meeting with a psychiatrist, as if the only thing he was likely to do with them was to sign some document of certification.

This type of consultant is actually an expert at putting people at ease and at listening to people's problems, and he has a sound working knowledge of all the latest forms of treatment. The net result of such an interview could well be advice to the family doctor as to how to carry on with treatment. Most general hospitals today have a psychiatric out-patient department. In our small town, the clinic is in the homely atmosphere of the cottage hospital. There are, of course, people who prefer a private consultation at the rooms of the consultant. For those who are excessively timid, a domiciliary visit by a psychiatrist and the general practitioner together can be arranged. We all feel more secure if we can meet people on our home ground. It is thus only rarely necessary for the sick person to have to visit a psychiatric hospital for a second opinion.

Today, very few patients need to be admitted to a psychiatric ward for treatment. This may, in fact, be in a general hospital, as most post-war hospitals contain a psychiatric unit. Furthermore, the psychiatric hospital itself is a very different place from what it used to be. I remember dealing with a woman who was very depressed, and under my care she was making painfully slow progress. It was *she* who asked *me* to get her transferred to a hospital. This was done, and when she returned home a few weeks later, she was quite a different woman. She had had exactly the same tablets in hospital as I had given her, and in precisely the same doses. I was frankly a bit puzzled by this, and when I asked her why she had improved in the ward and not at home, she told me that it was because life was so much easier for her in the new environment. She had shed all her responsibilities and could relax in a way she never could at home.

I once did a round in a children's hospital, and the paediatrician had admitted to his ward a tall boy of fourteen who had just lost his father. The huge lad seemed quite out of place among a lot of small children, and there was nothing physically wrong with him. I asked why he had been admitted. I was told that the boy had been extremely upset by the loss of his parent and the paediatrician had felt that it would not be easy for him to mourn and weep at home or at school without drawing attention to himself. While he was in hospital there was indeed no question of his going to school. The doctor had made a point of seeing him every day and together they discussed the situation and talked about the father. The idea was to help the boy to get the bitterness out of his system. When I remarked that I felt the doctor was making himself a father substitute, he replied that that was exactly what he was trying to do. I felt this was a splendid piece of medicine, and the temporary isolation from the painful environment which constantly reminded the boy of his father played a useful role in his recovery. This can indeed be one of the roles of a psychiatric hospital.*

Other Sources of Help

For one reason or another there are depressed people who are in need of help but who cannot bring themselves to consult the family doctor. There are, of course, other avenues open to them. The patient may be a woman who would prefer to talk to someone of her own sex. The practice nurse, who is a well-qualified and reliable member of the medical team, might be the person to consult. The State Registered Nurse (S.R.N.) is a highly qualified person who has usually spent some three years in training, and then another year or more gaining practical experience as a staff nurse in some hospital. A few have university degrees before they embark on their nursing career, and these graduate nurses are given every encouragement to enter this vocation by the authorities.

The State Enrolled Nurse (S.E.N.) has not the same experience or authority as the S.R.N., but many S.E.N.s have considerable experience of coping with people in psychological distress. Academic attainments and skill in coping with people are very different gifts. During the war there were a number of Red Cross Nurses, with a minimum of actual nursing experience, attached to our psychiatric unit. They were interested in this work and many of them did a first class job, even with the most disturbed patients. I have already pointed out that some doctors have the happy knack of rapidly being able to put the patient at her ease, and so acquire her confidence. The same thing applies to nurses. To some extent 'the listening ear' is a built-in characteristic of certain people who seem to have a larger than normal share of altruism and the ability to show genuine compassion. This useful faculty, like any other skill, is improved by practice.

Equally helpful is the Health Visitor (H.V.) who is a qualified nurse and midwife with special training in family welfare and child care. In addition to all the years spent in nursing, the H.V. has to undertake a long course to acquire the Health Visitor's Certificate. These people are quite used to

* Mr King, whose case history was given on page 41, was a similar case.

listening to people's problems and helping to solve them. If these nurses are unable to find some solution they will at least be able to recognize the need for further advice. If the sick person is scared of talking to her general practitioner, the intervention of a nurse or the H.V. can sometimes make the process a great deal easier, as the patient realizes that she has 'a friend in court'.

It may be that the melancholic wishes to get right away from the family doctor and his team at the health centre. If this happens there is the Social Services Department, of which there are offices in every area. Social Workers (S.W.s) are highly skilled persons, and they are experts in the art of counselling. If the patient wants to talk to a woman, this can be arranged. If she feels too ill to visit the office, a S.W. will make a house call. Modern S.W.s have wide fields of interest. They are skilled at sorting out many of the complex personal problems of the modern world in which we live. They can deal with such things as housing and the financial benefits and allowances due to single parent families. They understand the problems of child care, welfare for the aged, and how best to tackle the social ills of alcoholism and gambling. As with the general practitioner services, all that is discussed is a matter of complete confidence. In some areas there are S.W.s actually attached to general practices. This can be most helpful, but it is of little use to the sick person who wants to keep away from the family practice health centre.

If the family doctor has the advantage of being able to prescribe anti-depressant drugs, then the S.W.s are the experts in evaluating the importance of environment as a source of stress, and supplying the best remedies. I have already suggested that some people make a more rapid recovery from their troubles if they can accept the more relaxed atmosphere of a hospital, where they are relieved of all major responsibilities. The S.W.s can often do the same thing for the patients in their own homes, once the basis for the trouble has been identified, and the advantages of such possibilities are obvious. The skills of the S.W.s are different, and in some ways complementary, to those of the G.P. services. A few examples will illustrate the sort of problems the social services can handle so well.

Mrs Carter was the mother of five small children. Her husband who worked on the railway was found to have been pilfering parcels and equipment belonging to the firm. He was taken to the courts, found guilty, and given a three-month prison sentence. This family disgrace pushed Mrs Carter into a state of depression. She was utterly ashamed of what had happened and overwhelmed by the thought of having to care for the children on her own, with no prospect of a pay-packet for some months. She was dependent on the children's allowance, and a little social security for herself; she had never lived in such penury before.

A social worker was allocated to her case, and he found places in a day nursery for the pre-school children. He discovered that Mrs Carter was not really short of friends, and he arranged for kindly neighbours to transport her other children to and from their schools. Later, when she had had time to adjust, she was persuaded to travel with them and face up to the outside world, which was not nearly as hostile as she had imagined it to be. The S.W. made sure that she was collecting all the financial help that was due to her. This positive assistance, and the befriending by neighbours, carried her over the weeks her husband was away. Fortunately, he soon found work after his release, and the crisis was over.

Mr and Mrs Duffy had established themselves in the sheltered environment of an old people's flatlet, which had warden supervision. They were delighted with their new home, and their only child, a widowed daughter, lived nearby. She visited them regularly taking them a hot meal at midday twice a week. Unfortunately she fell ill, and cancer was diagnosed. As time passed she was able to do less and less for the old folk, and when she died, they were completely shattered. Mrs Duffy, who had for a long time been a little absent-minded, became a great deal worse, and the old man, who was deaf and only partially sighted, became little better. Their tidy little flatlet began to suffer, and both the doctor and the warden began to wonder what was going to happen to them.

A S.W. was invited to assess the situation. Meals on wheels were provided twice a week, and on the intervening days the home help called. She was able to tidy up the home, and cook a meal for them, as well as do the shopping when necessary. The same home help called each time, so that the old couple got used to her, and to some extent she became a daughter substitute. These two services went far to restore the morale of the old people, and together with the help and encouragement of the warden and many of their neighbours, they found they were better able to cope again, and they did more and more for themselves. They learned to make their own meals at the weekend and at other times when, for some reason, the home help could not attend.

Mrs Elton, a woman of forty, came to see me in great trouble. Her husband was becoming very suspicious of her, and accusing her of having a lover. If she threw a piece of paper in the fire, she was destroying a letter from her lover; and if a car hooted as it passed their house, the husband would rush to the window to see who it was, as he felt it was a signal from the lover to his wife. He was continuously questioning her, but nothing she could say would convince him that she had no interest in another man.

These symptoms sounded ominous to me, and I invited Mr Elton to come and see me. He brushed aside his wife's allegations and, as is usual in these situations, his story of what was happening was very different from hers. It was clear that unless some compromise could be reached, the marriage was in jeopardy. In this sort of case, where a couple are involved, I realize that I am usually prejudiced in favour of the woman; so to counter this tendency I asked a skilled woman S.W., who had been an ally of mine for many years, to make her assessment. She was an unmarried woman, about the same age as the disgruntled wife. She called at the house, and the problem was discussed over a cup of tea, with the woman on her own. She found that among other things, her client had taken to sleeping on the couch down stairs. The S.W. pointed out that if she continued to do this, it was small wonder that her fidelity was suspect; and she urged that it was imperative to resume normal marital relationships with her husband.

This advice, coming from a spinster, greatly impressed the woman. Various other suggestions were made to both parties, and when I discussed the case later with the S.W. I felt that her intervention had been more effective than anything I had done from the seclusion of my surgery. I do not imagine that the Elton marriage continued without its troubles, but a complete breakdown, with all its ill effects on the children, was averted. Ten years later, the couple were still together, and apparently reasonably adjusted.

These are just a few ways in which the social service workers can help. Of course, they have many other facilities and skills. They can assist the woman who is overwhelmed by the sheer size of her family and this, it has recently been shown, is a common basis for depression. Child-minders can be provided, school escorts found, as well as home-help assistance, to lessen the overall pressure of housework.

At the other end of the scale, they can assist in problems with the elderly. Mrs Low was being ground down by the stress of trying to run a home and family, and at the same time care for her aged and helpless old mother. The older woman was verging on the cabbage state and was quite unable to care for herself. Having graduated from the phase of needing baby-minders when they went out at night, the Lows now had to find a granny-sitter. The old woman was a pleasant old lady, but under the circumstances, Mrs Low's loyalty was strained to the utmost, and she felt that it was unfair on her husband. The social worker who was called in arranged for the old woman to attend a day hospital three times a week, and she was accommodated in an old people's home for a couple of weeks during the summer, to allow the Low family to get away together. These regular breaks away from looking after the older woman, made all the difference.

In the treatment of depressive illnesses, it is not always a case of seeing either a doctor or some member of the social services. These two organisations do not work in water-tight compartments, but they are in fact complementary services. When the Duffys lost their daughter and needed extra help in their flatlet, the G.P. called in a S.W. to assess the situation, and take any steps he thought necessary. In much the same way, if a S.W. feels there is a medical basis for the depression, as well as a complex social problem, the family doctor may well be called in to help.

The Church and the Samaritans

For those who belong to a church, there are today many vicars and members of religious bodies who have a great interest in people and their problems and have, as a result, developed facilities for helping those in trouble, no matter what the source. By the very nature of the illness, many melancholics must find their way to the confessional, or seek relief by consulting some minister of the Church. Many clergymen are now trained to be skilled therapists, and some have organized clinics and groups at which people with psychological problems are made welcome.

It was a clergyman, Chad Varah, who was so moved by the loneliness of many London city dwellers, that in 1953 he started the Samaritan organization, which now operates in every big town in Britain and in many other countries all over the world. This is a voluntary body dedicated to helping people in despair who just do not know which way to turn. It consists of groups of trained lay people directed by some expert. Should neither the facilities offered by the family doctor, nor the social services appeal to the sick person or her family, the Samaritan organization can be contacted by phone, at any hour of the day or night (the number of the nearest agency will be found in the telephone directory).

There is considerable reluctance on the part of most people to call in a doctor out of hours, and the offices of the social services may well be closed. The Samaritans are always available; the switchboard is constantly manned by trained volunteers who are eager to help those in trouble. It is not a substitute for medical psychiatric emergency services, but for the person who urgently wants to discuss some difficult emotional problem with a kindly and anonymous person, this service is ideal. The Samaritan who takes such a call may be able to help merely by talking the problem over there and then, but if it is in any way complicated he will arrange an early interview with the most appropriate advisor. If the case is especially urgent, a home visit may be fixed up within the hour. The sick person is assured of a sympathetic hearing, the advice of an expert if that is necessary, and every effort will be made to sort out the problem. One of the most attractive facilities put forward by this body is a system of befriending.

For a limited period of time, the lonely and perhaps confused person, is assured of the support and friendship of a worker allocated to help her. Other melancholics may find their way to the facilities offered by self-help organizations, and these will be described in some detail in the last chapter.

Few of the medical fraternity will object if some of their depressed patients seek help from outside bodies. If thereby they can find some solution to their problems, so much the better; but in some cases, medical intervention is essential. I was once contacted on the telephone by a worried and embarrassed Samaritan from the nearest town. He had been confronted by a patient of mine who was clearly disturbed and in urgent need of medical help. She had sought assistance from him, and he in turn needed advice from me. He happened to know I had a special interest in depression as he had attended a lecture I had given a month before. With a little tact, co-operation and good will, it was not too difficult to sort this problem out.

Non-medical organizations are usually well able to deal with depressions which are reactive in origin. However, if any of the lay-therapists are confronted by a melancholic suffering from endogenous depression, no matter whether this be a primary type, or secondary due to severe mental trauma, they can be in difficulties. Such a client needs medical help from some source. As I have indicated, endogenous depression is one of the easiest forms of melancholia to treat. The fact that some of these patients seek help away from the doctors underlines one important principle. These sick people need a great deal of support and encouragement as well as medical treatment.

Chapter 5
Psychotherapy

In the middle of the last century, scientific medicine flourished as never before and doctors came to feel that there was a clear-cut explanation of all human ills. The microscope enabled them to examine tissues from the body, so that they were actually able to see the changes brought about by disease processes. They also found, in some cases, the micro-organisms that had caused the trouble.

Side by side with these discoveries, the conviction grew that, having found the cause, a cure for the malady was just round the corner, and so research was intensified and medicine became more and more scientific. However, one group of illnesses defied such explanations. These were the psychoneurotic complaints. Many of the grossest forms of mental illness, which afflicted the vast majority of the patients crowded into the Victorian lunatic asylums, showed no pathological changes in the brain after death. The most searching examination of the cerebral tissues of those who had actually died in depression, mania, or suffering from schizophrenia, showed no microscopic changes which could in any way account for the symptoms. The neurotic illnesses called by many names such as the vapours, hysteria, or hypochondriasis, were non-lethal diseases; but if the killer complaints showed no tissue changes, there was little chance of any pathological explanation being found in these so-called minor troubles.

This was indeed a baffling situation, and as so often happens when something cannot be understood, it was laid aside and the mainstream of scientific medicine flowed on around it. While the florid cases of the major psychoses continued to be accepted as genuine if unfortunate illnesses, to be hidden from the public eye as far as possible in remote asylums, the minor upsets we now call psychoneuroses or anxiety states were said to have a moral basis. They were attributed to weakness of character, cowardice or lack of moral fibre. From this sprang the modern attitude I have already described, in which this type of illness is viewed as something vaguely disgraceful.

Freud

There were, however, a few pioneers who sought for different explanations and remedies, and the greatest of these was an Austrian physician, Sigmund Freud. He devised a new method of both interpretation and treatment called psycho-analysis. In brief, the patient had to visit the therapist five times a week for an hour at a time. She lay relaxed on a couch, and by a process called free association her psychological problems were slowly unravelled. The hope was that although it might take years to achieve, the patient would in the end discover where in infancy and early life her psychic development had gone wrong, and the whole mental structure would be rebuilt from there in a more stable and mature way. The patient would thus emerge from psycho-analysis a new and thoroughly balanced individual, able to understand herself, and cope with any future adversity in life without having to take refuge in neurotic illness.

Such treatment was, of course, time-consuming, and very expensive, and so quite beyond the reach of all but the very rich. Looking back over the best part of a century of psycho-analysis, most authorities today will agree that Freud, and even more his over-enthusiastic supporters, have overplayed their case, and that the treatment was, in fact, by no means the unqualified success they claimed it to be. Freud's great contributions to the problem were that he boldly tackled an important side of medicine that was being neglected and he discovered valid explanations of certain psychiatric illnesses and some aspects of human behaviour. Unhappily, the under-standing of the cause of an illness does not produce an immediate cure, but this was just what the world of Freud's day was expecting. A famous German contemporary of his, Robert Koch, by means of a most elegant piece of research, discovered the causal organism of tuberculosis, which at that time was such a scourge throughout the whole world it was called the white plague. Having discovered the germ, everyone thought that a cure would very soon be found, but it was another sixty years before an effective remedy for this killer disease was available.

Freud's psycho-analysis was indeed no cure-all for psychoneurosis, and before he died he himself predicted that a chemical basis for mental illness would be discovered some day, and this he felt would revolutionize treatment. In the meantime, he maintained, psycho-analysis was the best remedy available. If the efficacy of these measures has been exaggerated, this must not detract from the value of psychotherapy as such. There are simpler and less time-consuming measures.

A Helping Hand

Faced by an adverse environment, in most instances the victim is able to work her way through the bad patch and outside help is unnecessary. We must all have seen this happen when there has been a death in the family. The bitterness of mourning makes the victim sad and miserable; family and friends rally round, and most people are soon able to carry on with a normal kind of routine once the funeral is over. However, each one of us has a breaking point, even the toughest individual, and there are inevitably some casualties who are overwhelmed by their misfortunes.

Such people need a helping hand of some kind, to help them to adjust and come to terms with their difficulties. Generally speaking the adviser must have training and experience in counselling, but this form of treatment is by no means confined to the medical profession. As we have seen, social workers, psychologists, clergy and teachers can all play a part. Sometimes talking out a problem with a sympathetic listener is enough, especially if the listener shows unexpected concern.

An old pitman told me how in 1934 he lost his only son down the mine, when the lad was only fifteen. He was heart-broken and paralysed with grief, but somehow he managed to struggle back to work. He told me that he did not know what would have happened to him if a certain fellow had not come to his aid. This chap sought him out at work one day, and asked him to drop everything and come for a walk with him. They wandered away from the mine across some fields. His companion got him to unburden himself of all fearful sorrow, and assured him that all his friends and workmates shared his distress. For an hour they talked as if time did not matter, and nothing was as important as just listening to the mourner's story, and showing that he, the listener, and everyone else, really cared.

At last they returned to the pit, and before he went back to his job, the pitman was told he could seek another talk at any time he liked. However, this single session has made him feel different, and he was able to face life again. I was most impressed by this story and I asked him who his companion had been. He told me it was the colliery manager himself, and it was clear that his timely concern, and his skill in what can be called man-management, had been a turning point in the process of this man's grief.

The Human Element
In the same way, and quite apart from formal psychotherapy, the importance of sympathetic handling of the patient cannot be over emphasized; it is an essential part of all good medicine. It is an integral part of the technique employed by herbalists, Nature Curers, and other practitioners of so-called fringe medicine, and to some extent this accounts for some of their success in treatment. The modern doctor has so many powerful physical remedies available, he sometimes tends to rely on science, to the exclusion of man-management.

This trend is most unfortunate. I would suggest that the best medicine is a mixture of 60 per cent science and 40 per cent art. By art I mean the ability to understand people, to listen to them, and inspire them with confidence. This means becoming to some extent emotionally involved. The therapist, by understanding the problem, suffers with the patient, who is aware this is happening. In an earlier chapter, I described how a paediatrician had laid himself out to be a father substitute for a boy who had lost his father. In much the same way, the therapist may for a time supply the moral support and encouragement that a recently widowed woman could have expected from her husband.

Patients of all kinds tend to think that they are alone with their troubles, and it is this sense of isolation which has in part prompted the creation of so many self-help groups like Alcoholics Anonymous, Parkinson's Disease Society, the Colostomy Welfare Group, and many others. Sick people can derive considerable comfort from talking to fellow sufferers about problems they have in common. Many doctors are aware of what help can be derived from such contacts.

A friend of mine was advised to have his bladder removed because of a serious cancer problem, and it was clearly going to be a major operation. The surgeon who was going to carry out the operation asked a patient who had had the same operation seven years before to call and talk to my friend. This session with a fellow sufferer did far more good than any amount of talking and explanation by experts. The patient was also impressed by the surgeon's thoughtfulness in arranging such a meeting. I used the same technique for patients who were fearful to have a course of electroplexy (E.C.T.). I found that their apprehension could often be allayed by talking to a recovered melancholic who had had such treatment successfully in the past.

Reluctance to Talk

Patients suffering from depression often feel more cut off from others than most patients, and they are less inclined to discuss their troubles. There are, of course, exceptions: some melancholics just cannot stop talking about their problems. The reluctance to talk is the old story of feeling ashamed of themselves; the conviction that the illness is in some way their own fault. So often the patient also lacks energy, and they find it hard to make the effort. The patient may know he has changed in some way; and if with a supreme effort he drags himself to the local pub for his usual pint, he may be upset by remarks from his buddies. Someone is almost bound to point out that he is unusually quiet, and then ask him outright what is wrong. He just cannot stand this kind of questioning, so he stops going down to the local. Shakespeare described this situation very clearly: 'Thus misery doth part the flux in company.'

The melancholic does indeed tend to feel both isolated and misunderstood by all and sundry. For most of us, the very human need for sympathetic understanding and support is satisfied by the stable marriage relationship, where hopes and fears can be discussed in an atmosphere of mutual trust. Communications of this kind are not confined to speech: they can be passed on by a knowing glance, a wink, or even a kick under the table. All these things enhance the bond between man and wife. It is not surprising to find, as Brown and Harris[1] have pointed out, that when this bond disappears both partners are placed in a potentially vulnerable situation. More will be said on this point later.

The Catholic Church has always made good use of this technique. The value and helpfulness of the one-to-one interview by way of the confessional has survived the centuries, and most people who have made use of it know how helpful it can be. To be really effective, the priest and his parishioner must be well acquainted. Car drives are excellent places for useful talks of this kind. Little of any significance is said between individuals at a party, for instance, but much useful work can be done by the confidential talks that take place in a car. I once offered a lift to a patient waiting at a bus stop. She told me she had been wanting to see me for weeks, but just could not pluck up her courage. She had a lump in her breast, and took little persuasion to see me at the surgery that evening.

Professional Help
People with problems they cannot solve for themselves, nor find relief by discussing things with the family or friends, certainly need professional help by way of psychotherapy or counselling. There are many ways in which this process can help the client, and each therapist has his own techniques. It would be impossible to describe them all, but they all have certain principles in common which were listed by Medawar.[2]

He suggested that the patient must be seen at regular intervals by a sympathetic listener who was prepared to take all complaints seriously. Secondly, the therapist should be at pains to point out that the problem of psychoneurosis was not unusual, but indeed shared by many other people. Lastly, the symptoms and the mechanism of the illness must be explained to the patient in terms she can understand. This last stage is a combination of reassurance, explanation, and interpretation. This sort of procedure takes time, and for this reason, psychotherapy is not always available on the National Health Service. There are indeed some G.P.s who practise it, and it is also used in one form or another in the psychiatric services, but the supply of therapists is always well behind the demand. It is because of this deficiency that the churches and other bodies have taken to training interested people to become counsellors.

For most people it is not easy to discuss intimate problems with another person. The process is comparable with the act of getting stripped completely naked for a medical examination; the whole performance is embarrassing, and the person who lies nude on the couch inevitably feels in rather a vulnerable situation. Divesting 'psychological clothes' can be equally disconcerting. The whole process of psychotherapy is an uncomfortable procedure; if it is just a pleasant social chat, it is unlikely to do much good. The trouble is that few of us enjoy seeing ourselves as we really are. We are rarely satisfied by how we look in a photograph, or our appearance as seen from some unusual angle in a mirror, and I have never yet found anyone who likes the sound of his own voice on a tape recorder. Probing into personal problems is in many ways comparable to the above situations. It is painful while it lasts and we do not like what emerges. However, as with many forms of treatment, the patient has to feel worse before she feels better. The victim of a hernia who goes into hospital to have it repaired feels far more uncomfortable just after the operation than before it took place. In time the discomfort passes, and in the long term the patient benefits.

As in all difficult situations, it does help if one knows what is going to happen, and so I will now describe the steps I would take with a patient who came to see me with a problem. The first step is to listen to the patient's story, and give her every encouragement to open up, to say all she can about her troubles. The history of the case is taken in detail. A note is made of what illnesses she has had in the past and, if there have been other episodes of nervous troubles, the nature of the break-down is recorded. It is important to take a family history: Are the parents still alive? What is the patient's attitude to them? How many siblings does she have? Where does she come in the family tree? It is most important to know precisely when the illness started if this date can be given. The background as well as the story itself is of great importance. A psychiatrist has been described as a doctor who can record a good case history, and it is indeed very important.

In 1978 Brown and Harris[3] evolved an important thesis. They pointed out that there are three factors in the life of a woman which render her particularly vulnerable to depression. The first is a breakdown in the lines of communication between her and her husband, so that they cannot freely discuss mutual problems. The second is the loss of her own mother before the age of eleven (this could be by way of death or by separation). The third item is when a woman has to care for three or more children under the age of fourteen. The first two of these three factors apply equally to men, although it does seem from the statistics that men are not as sensitive to depressive syndromes as women. These authors went on to propose that if all three disposing factors were present and the woman was confronted by some added crisis, such as the loss of a close friend, then a depressive episode was inevitable.

It is important to know when exactly the illness starts. It may stem from some particular event; the patient may realize that she has never felt normal since an attack of influenza, or since the birth of her last baby. On the other hand, the start may have been so insidious, that it is difficult to name a precise time. It is also important to know if there are any drugs which could possibly be a basis for the symptoms.

Having done all this, I as a doctor always undertook a complete physical examination, to exclude any organic disease. If a lay-therapist is dealing with a patient, and any physical illness is suspected, it is wise to refer the patient to her G.P. for a physical check-up. This medical procedure serves a number of useful purposes. The patient may be worried about some illness she dare not mention, and a reassuring verdict after the examination often helps (anyone who has passed a check up for an insurance policy knows the feeling of relief). The more thorough the examination, the more it helps to build up the rapport with the patient. No stone is being left unturned, and the patient feels that the doctor is indeed taking her complaint seriously.

Talking through the Problem

Having excluded organic disease and other causes for the depression, formal therapeutic sessions are initiated, in which both the client and her counsellor try to sort out her problem. In rare cases it is completely soluble. Mrs Jones came to see me with her small boy who had impetigo. Having dealt with this problem, and just before she left the consulting room, she asked me if she could have some sleeping tablets. I brought her back and explained that these alone would solve nothing, and I asked her if she knew why she was not sleeping. She admitted that the basis was some domestic trouble, so I asked her to make a long appointment to see me the next day.

At that session she told me that her husband was becoming more and more estranged. They had been fond of dancing, but the pleasure had gone from this, as he seemed jealous if she danced with other men. He was all the time carping about trivialities, and he had never been like it before.

When I heard her story, I asked her if her husband would be likely to come and see me himself, and she agreed to ask him. She had no objection to my discussing with him any of the things she had told me. He came to see me, and when I told him his wife's story he became quite upset in a rather unexpected way. He had had no idea he had been so querulous, and on reflection realized that he had been particularly hard pressed at work, and dissatisfied with the job. Without realizing it, he had been taking his basic irritation out on his wife. He told me that already he had been appointed to a new post which he felt would suit him better.

That simple intervention by a third party who had the confidence of both sides did the trick. There was never any need to prescribe tablets.

Needless to say, the problem is usually much more difficult to solve. The woman who is depressed because her husband has died has no easy solution to her problem: the best she can hope for is to come to terms with her single state. In most cases the family and friends supply all the help that is needed, but just occasionally specialist support is necessary. Counselling may help her to understand the mechanism of mourning, and to realize that some of the symptoms which frighten her are commonplace and normal to bereaved people.

For instance, sometimes on waking she may feel that her husband is standing at the foot of the bed. She knows the sensation is false and misleading, although she wishes it was true. She may well feel it is a symptom indicating that she is going out of her mind. To be told that this is thoroughly normal, and that others have those feelings, is a great comfort. Torrie[4] has written an excellent short book designed to help such women. For the general reader, a monograph by Murray-Parkes[5] is advocated. This psychiatrist has made a study of bereavement and mourning over many years, and in his book he describes the mechanism very clearly.

Sometimes the mere act of discussing the problem can help the patient to make the best of things. Mrs MacKay came to see me because she was unhappy about her sex life. She had been married for fifteen years and she had three fine sons. She was at first embarrassed by what she had to say. When she and her husband were courting, he was very loving and affectionate, kissing her a great deal. After years of marriage, he had dropped all the trappings. If he wanted intercourse at night, there were no preliminaries. He just took what he wanted, rolled over and in a few seconds was sound asleep, while his wife wept into her pillow with frustration. The husband came to see me and I discussed the matter with him, but he really had no idea what I was talking about, and when all three of us discussed the sex act it was the same.

Finally, his wife came to see me on her own. She thanked me for what I had tried to do, and said that after due consideration she realized that things could be a lot worse.

Her man was a good worker and they were comfortably off. He did not drink and they had three fine children, so she had decided to accept the situation and make the best of it. Another factor probably helped her, although she did not mention it: the discussion of the situation had made her realize that her expectations from her husband were not unreasonable; that she was not a sex maniac. To talk over such an intimate matter with a man, and win his approval of her attitude, had been a great consolation. In this imperfect world, many of us, like Mrs MacKay, have to compromise and make the best of the situation as it is.

Some brave people work out their own solution. Mrs Mason was a childless married woman of about fifty. Married for over twenty years, she was in great distress because her husband, who was a business executive, wanted her to divorce him so that he could go off with his pretty young secretary. I listened to her story and made sympathetic noises. Her husband was unwilling to discuss the matter with any outside agency. Mrs Mason had a strong personality, and more courage than most people. After a couple of sessions with me, she decided on her own plan of action. She told her husband that she would never agree to a divorce, but that if he wanted to go off with his girl-friend, she was willing to allow this for six months. They would then hold a further discussion on the matter.

One month later, her husband was only too glad to come home and be cared for by one who knew all his idiosyncrasies, and could accept them. The secretary found a new job! This strategy was not devoid of risks, and could never have been suggested by a third party, but in this case it worked well. Shock tactics invented and applied by the aggrieved person do sometimes work.

Seeing Things in Proportion
Often the patient is too close to her problems to appreciate what the trouble really is all about. If you hold a page of this book close to your eyes you will be aware of the print, but you cannot read a line. If you take the page away, the type comes clearly into focus. This is analogous to psychotherapy; the therapist helps his client to see things more clearly and in proportion. Sometimes the sick person is not really aware of

the basis for her symptoms, and to identify the problem she needs help.

Miss Newman was the personal secretary to a business tycoon. She was engaged to a young man who had a good job at the local council offices and they were saving hard to get married. She began to have palpitations and was sure she had a bad heart. She felt she would really never live long enough to reach the altar. There was no evidence of any heart disease and together we could find no basis for her worry, so among other suggestions she was asked to record her dreams. She came along with a most helpful sample. She and her fiancé were in the dream, house-hunting. As is so common these days, there was little to choose from, only two places in fact. The first was a council house, adequate but quite unimaginative. The second was a huge mansion of a place, a dream palace quite beyond their means. When asked if she knew of anyone who lived in such luxury, she said it was like her boss's home.

The choice implication of the dream was obvious; she was in a state of indecision between two men, her council clerk and her employer. When she thought it over, she realized that the latter was making friendly approaches, and that subconsciously she was attracted to him. Once she had faced up to the situation, she found a new job, and a year later she married her fiancé. With these counselling sessions her heart fears left her. The camouflage of heart disease was of course most appropriate, and this kind of thing is called by some 'organ language'.

Worry and Physical Illness

Some people like Miss Newman became so convinced they have some bodily disease, it is very hard to reassure them. Attempts to do so often evoke a resentful response to the implication that the patient has imagined it all. Even when symptoms are real they can easily be misinterpreted. If you have nearly walked under a bus, and the driver shouts abuse at you, you may well be conscious of a fluttering in your chest, but this does not bother you simply because you know the reason for it. You have had a fright; you are acutely embarrassed and this had brought on the sensation.

If, however, for no apparent reason, the heart flutters, the patient is quite understandably worried, and she thinks of heart disease with all its possible consequences. The mere worrying about some problem raises tension and can make the heart flutter, as it did with Miss Newman. There are many who do not appreciate that this can happen, but the influence of mind over matter is stronger than we sometimes realize.

If you go to a party and find that you have forgotten your handkerchief, at once your nose will begin to run, even if you do not have a cold. The very thought that you cannot blow your nose just when you want to makes it drip. A few paper handkerchiefs borrowed from your host and your troubles are at an end. Most people have at some time had this experience and can appreciate its significance.

In much the same way we all know that if we have to walk across a room with people staring at us, there is a tendency to fall over ones feet. There are, in fact, many functions, like walking, swallowing, or breathing, that are done best if we do not think about them. Those who concentrate on the act of breathing can upset it; the smooth, even rhythm becomes uneven, and the victim begins to sigh, gets tight feelings in the chest, and wonders if the breathing will stop altogether. This, of course, only makes her feel worse, and a vicious circle of discomfort is set up. The harder she works on her breathing, the more uncomfortable it gets. These breathing fears may make the patient feel very uncomfortable, but she can do herself no harm. The best thing to do is to try and relax, to breath *slowly* and evenly. Some distraction like television can be helpful, and with such measures the feelings soon pass.

Worry, then, cannot in itself produce disease, but it readily brings on symptoms which suggest physical illness to the patient. People often think that shock can bring on an illness quite out of the blue, but this is not true. Yet while some severe psychic trauma cannot itself cause serious disease, it can be the last straw, so that some impending condition can become manifest. A young man of twenty-seven had a car crash in which a woman was killed. He himself was not badly hurt and he was exonerated from all blame, but a week later he became a florid diabetic. It seems likely that he would have developed diabetes in any case, but the accident, and the stress engendered from it, made it evident a few weeks or months before it would otherwise have appeared. While stress alone does not cause organic illness, it can intensify symptoms of disease that are already present. Diabetics quickly learn that worry has a bad effect on control, and they know they will need more insulin during a period of crisis.

Stress can also elevate blood pressure to a dangerous level. The famous surgeon, John Hunter, who suffered from angina, told his friends that his life was in the hands of any knave who cared to upset him, thereby implying that an emotional upset could bring on a fatal heart attack. His prediction was correct. An irascible character, Hunter had a violent quarrel at a board meeting and this precipitated a fatal attack of angina.

Psychotherapeutic Addiction

While few would dispute the help that psychotherapy can give to patients, there are certain dangers attached to such treatment. The first thing to bear in mind is that it can become addictive.

Mrs Deacon was a middle-aged woman with a large teenage family. Her father died and she found herself having to look after her widowed mother. The newcomer to the household was no easy guest, and there was considerable friction in the family. Mrs Deacon struggled to keep the peace, and she felt ashamed that she could not manage things better. Her strong ambivalent attitude to her mother was a source of considerable distress. Being a member of a lively church, she approached her vicar, who was an experienced therapist, and she found considerable comfort from the counselling sessions she had with him.

After a few weeks she realized she was becoming dependent on these interviews and with his concurrence she stopped the treatment, although it had helped her a great deal. For the next few weeks she had a reaction, which was like giving up smoking.

It takes insight and courage to act like this and to make the break at the correct time. Others become hooked on psychotherapy as securely as other unfortunate folk become addicted to drugs. A bright medical student, who was clearly destined to go far in his profession, became obsessed with the idea that he was a homosexual, and the idea appalled him. He sought the help of a Freudian psycho-analyst, and for the next fifteen years he had five sessions a week of expensive therapy. It also meant that his freedom of movement was curtailed, as he had to find a job that would fit in with his treatment sessions.

In the end, the therapist died, and after a stormy period of deep mourning, the patient recovered and married a few years later. There were no children to the union. For this individual, the treatment was a great help, and if it could have been cut off after a reasonable interval of time, I would have been full of praise for its efficacy. However, it went on so long that the bond between the patient and the therapist was too strong to be healthy. Nobody has the right to be so completely dependent on another individual, and this applies even to the husband and wife situation. They share the most important pair-bonding in our social structure, but if, when bereavement comes, as come it must, the survivor becomes pathologically depressed, then the bonding has become too secure for mental maturity.

Natural Remission
One more pitfall with this form of treatment, is when recovery has been due to the natural remission of the illness. Man is a most resilient creature, and all through his history he has thrived on finding a way round difficulties. The sting of even the most severe trauma passes. However, there is a place for supportive treatment. It may not produce a subtle, satisfying explanation of what has caused the illness, but the patient is sustained by the sympathy and encouragement of the therapist. This is what is needed in dealing with cases of endogenous depression.

Until physical treatment has relieved the low moods, the patient needs regular and sustained help. There may be questions to answer, and fears to allay. In the past I was often taken in by this type of illness. I remember one woman who was having regular sessions of psychotherapy because of some marital problem and under my care she made a good recovery. At the time I felt most gratified at the success of my therapy. However, as the years rolled by, and she kept reappearing at the surgery with a succession of depressive episodes and I realized the original 'cure' had been no more than a natural remission of an illness.

Some anxious people also grasp at the support of a sympathetic listener, to help them through a crisis. Mrs Bird came to see me with a whole string of symptoms which I accepted as evidence of her anxiety and she then came for regular sessions of treatment. One morning she arrived in high spirits, and she told me she had recovered and would not need to take up any more of my time. Having thanked me for all my encouragement and help, she asked me if I knew the basis for her worry. Glancing at her case notes I made a few suggestions, but she brushed them all aside. Then she explained her problem. 'My mother died of cancer at the age of thirty-nine, I am forty today, and I haven't a care in the world.'

Convinced that she was going to die like her mother at thirty-nine, she sought help from a sympathetic listener, and leaned on him until the crisis had passed. Without knowing how or why, I had in some way helped her, just as I consciously and deliberately set out to support the melancholic through her bad patches.

In Freudian and many of the earlier forms of psychotherapy, the therapist delved back into the past, and attempted to lay the blame on remote events, at the same time trying to reconstruct the patients's attitude along what was thought to be more mature lines. If we care to look back, all of us have some skeletons in the cupboard, and brooding over them does no good. It may explain, but it does not cure. This thesis has been rejected by some modern psychiatrists who suggest that patients must look to the future and not the past. What has happened cannot be reversed; it cannot be forgotten, but it must be accepted. Dwelling on our misfortunes is a sterile exercise. It is the patients' attitude to the future that matters. I endorse this view.

No mention has been made of drug treatment, and this is because I have been trying to explain the place of what some people regard as the 'talking treatment', as applied to cases of reactive depression and anxiety states in general. The place of drugs will be dealt with in the next chapter, but I would emphasize here that there is no medicament yet invented that is as useful in the treatment of worry as a sympathetic ear.

Notes

[1] G.W. Brown and T. Harris, *Social Origins of Depression*. Tavistock Press, 1978.

[2] P.B. Medawar, *The Art of the Soluble*. Methuen, 1967.

[3] G.W. Brown and T. Harris, *op. cit.*

[4] M. Torrie, *Begin Again*. Dent, 1970.

[5] C. Murray-Parkes, *Bereavement*. Penguin, 1973.

Chapter 6
Physical Methods of Treatment

I had been interested in depressive disorders for some fourteen years before any effective drug treatment became available to me as a G.P. Drugs had been developed sporadically, but none of them had been very helpful. Amphetamine products had offered the best hope, but the side-effects had militated against them. They increased the problem of insomnia, and patients tended to feel tense or even agitated, and only marginally more cheerful or comfortable. The best agent, dubbed with the name of 'purple hearts', was the most effective, but it turned out to be highly addictive. There was indeed no satisfactory remedy available.

Today there are so many potent drugs on hand that we tend to feel that there is an appropriate tablet to cure every condition and every disease. This rather naive attitude is of course over-sanguine; the pendulum of what can be called 'the drug explosion' has gone too far in the direction of optimism. However, one has to have lived and worked in the age before they were available to appreciate fully the advantages that have accrued from the sensible use of psychotropic drugs.

Before 1958 the situation was as follows. If the depressed patient was in a bad way, retarded or agitated, then treatment in the form of electroplexy at the local mental hospital was available. If, however, the sick person suffered from a mild or moderate depression very little could be done. Insomnia was treated by giving powerful hypnotics at night, but these often had a hangover effect and made the patient feel more depressed than ever in the mornings. The patient was supported by regular consultations, during which she was assured she was suffering from an illness that would pass. She was told there were many people like her and that no matter how low she felt recovery would occur in time. These unhappy people appeared to be quite incredulous at the time, but once they were better many told me how much this constant reassurance had helped. The fact that they kept on coming to see me in spite of feeling so weak and ill, was in itself evidence that these sessions were valuable.

The Advent of Drugs
Towards the end of the 1950s I eagerly read the literature of new agents that were on trial at the time, and when I was given the opportunity of trying some of the new drugs on my patients I was very ready to do so. I had a long list of suitable candidates. Mr Ottey, for instance, had been a typical manic-depressive patient since the age of twenty-two, and he had been in and out of mental institutions most of his working life. On the death of his wife, he returned to our village to live with his elderly parents. When I first saw him he was in a state of chronic depression. An architect by profession, work was quite out of the question, he could not settle to read, he did little about the house, and seemed to spend all his days sitting in a chair by the fire. He would not consider seeing a psychiatrist, or returning to a mental hospital for more electroplexy.

However, when drugs were available to me he told me he was quite agreeable to try the tablets, but he admitted that he had little faith in them. Ten days after starting his course, much to my surprise, he appeared at the surgery. I had never seen him out of the house before. He had come armed with plans of a new bungalow he was going to have built for himself. These were all drawn up with the meticulous accuracy of an expert. I felt I was expected to make some comments and so, adding to my approval of his scheme, I suggested a few minor alterations. He was back again at the evening surgery with new plans which had incorporated my ideas. The complete transformation in this man was unbelievable. The drug had certainly relieved his depression. There were many others like him.

Mrs Povey was a married woman of fifty-two. She suffered from depression during the war which had been severe enough to take her into the local mental hospital. After a spell of several months there, she returned home, but she was far from well; she was a typical case of an arrested depression. She could run the home and look after her husband, but no more. I offered her the opportunity to try the new tablets, and she was quite willing to accept them. Within a month she was a different woman, happy and as active as she had been before her wartime illness had started. She resumed work in the garden, rejoined the Women's Institute, and went to church on Sundays with her husband, things she had not done for fifteen years.

These cases, and many others besides, convinced me that at last we had a chemical agent which could really help patients with *certain types* of depression. The one most likely to respond was the primary endogenous depression, of which Mr Ottey, the architect, was a good example. The second type of case to do well was the reactive depression that was so severe it had acquired many of the symptoms of endogenous depression, the category I have called the secondary endogenous-like depression. Mrs Robson was the mother of four children. They were all very good looking, and she thought the world of them. She was a good housewife and ran her home very well. When the youngest child, a pretty little girl, was about a year old, she was found to be congenitally deaf and, on questioning, it was discovered that Mrs Robson had had German measles in the early weeks of her pregnancy. The discovery of this defect in a member of the family of which she was so proud was too much for her and she became completely obsessed with her troubles. She blamed herself; she should have been more careful when she was carrying the child, and she certainly should never have visited a brother whose family had German measles. Repeated therapeutic sessions were a waste of time and ideas of self blame continued to go round and round in her head. She was given anti-depressant drugs and she began to improve. She learned to accept things as they were, and started to look round to see what could be done for the child, and how under the circumstances the girl could get the best education. Any case of reactive depression which fails to respond to counselling should be tried on anti-depressant drugs, as what appears to be anxiety can be an endogenous type of depression in disguise.

Main Types of Drugs

There are today three main types of drug for the treatment of depression. Without going into the complicated details of how they are supposed to act on certain centres in the brain, it is useful to know something about them.

The Tricyclic Group

The first drugs I used in the cases I have described belonged to the tricyclic group: Tofranil or Tryptizol are examples of this agent. As a rule these medicaments take ten to fourteen days to act, and it is usually six weeks before the patient is completely back to normal. The whole course may last anything from three months to a year. As a 'rule of thumb' I used to suggest that for patients under thirty, the course would last for three months; if they were over thirty it would take six months. There were of course many individual variations. This may seem to be an awful long time. In the first place the patient has to wait a couple of weeks for any improvement, and then a matter of months before the tablets can be stopped. Let me repeat what happened before there were any potent drugs. The *average* duration of the illness was about eleven months, and the patient felt wretched and ill the whole of that time. The melancholic is far better off today.

Side-effects

The tricyclic drugs give the patient a dry mouth, and it may be difficult to focus with the eyes. In some elderly men, bladder function may be upset. If these symptoms are too severe, the patient or a relative should report them to the doctor, but *the dosage should not be changed without seeking his instructions*.

These side-effects are usually not unbearable, and they lessen with time. The usual practice is to give large doses of the tablets at night: this helps the patient to sleep, and by morning the worst symptoms have worn off. There is considerable variation in the dosage: some people improve on small amounts, and others need a great deal more. In general, the bigger the dose, the quicker the recovery.

Alcohol tends to be potentiated by all psychotropic drugs; this means that a single whisky acts like a double. Alcohol is probably best avoided or only taken in very small amounts and always with caution. Similarly, the drug may make the patient feel continually sleepy, in which case driving a car should be firmly discouraged.

Moods may also oscillate, and this can be very disconcerting. After a few days the patient feels a little better, and hope rises, but then the next day she feels worse than ever. If the patient realizes this can happen, and that it is evidence that the depression is breaking up, she can usually take it, but it can be very trying. It only lasts for a few days. Once the two week plateau has been reached, these mood swings tend to drop off.

M.A.O. Group

The second group of drugs are known as the monoamineoxydase inhibitors. (M.A.O.) The first of these drugs was a product called iproniazid. Initially it was used in conjunction with other agents in the treatment of pulmonary tuberculosis, and this particular drug was found to produce a state of euphoria in the patient. A psychiatrist who noticed this reaction realized its possibilities, and tried it on depressed patients, and in some cases the good response was quite dramatic. After a few days of treatment, the low moods just faded away, and the patient returned to a normal state of well being, or even moved into hypomania.

One of my patients who reacted in this way expressed her feelings of increased activity by saying she was so busy and energetic that she was beginning to meet herself coming back. These drugs do not suit every patient, but when they do work the patient responds rather more quickly than with the tricyclic group of drugs.

M.A.O. therapy can bring the patient back to a level of well-being unknown for years. The patient most likely to respond best is when the melancholia has assumed a picture of hypochondrical ruminations, or the patient has phobic symptoms such as a fear of open spaces, or overcrowding, and while the response may be most gratifying, the drug may well have to be taken over a long stretch of time.

Mr Gadsby was a married man in his early forties. He was hard-working and he held a responsible job at the local pit. Work on the surface was easy for him, but he hated going down the mine; the cage ride was sheer agony to him. Crowds and closed spaces also upset him. A religious man, he often missed services as he dreaded the confined atmosphere of the chapel. When he was given M.A.O. drugs there was a dramatic improvement. The treatment, he said, had made a new man of him. He became a regular chapel-goer, and found he could do and enjoy things he had avoided for years. Going down the pit ceased to worry him. When he came once for a repeat prescription, I warned him that he would have to take the tablets for quite a time. He replied that the improvement was such that if it meant taking them for the rest of his life he would be happy to do so. As with the tricyclic drugs there are possible side effects.

Side-effects

Iproniazid, the drug first used, was found sometimes to cause liver damage, but today there are much safer and better M.A.O. agents. The main side-effect of the tablets is that they sometimes react with an amino acid called tyramine, which is found in certain types of food, and the net result of this can be a bad headache. The foods to be avoided include cheese, marmite, herring roes, broad beans, and red wine, especially Chianti. This phenomenon is now well recognized, and if M.A.O. drugs are prescribed the patient is given a small card with a list of the food items which are forbidden. It is important to adhere to these restrictions, but I must point out that only a minority of patients are likely to react in this way. I mention this because people who eat restricted foods in error do tend to panic. If by mistake a cheese sandwich is eaten, the chances are that nothing untoward will happen, and if it does occur, the doctor has a remedy.

Before we knew about the so called 'cheese reaction', I had

treated scores of patients with these drugs, and I only had five such reactions, none of which were serious. Since patients were advised as to the correct diet, I have had none, just a few worried patients who by mistake had eaten a forbidden item, and none of them had any trouble. If the recovered melancholic, who is still on M.A.O. drugs goes to a dinner party, the restrictions can be an embarrassment. I would suggest that the odd glass of white wine is taken and sipped slowly. When it comes to the cheese course, a small portion can be taken and simply left on the plate. This causes far less attention than making a point about cheese being a forbidden item.

I have already mentioned the danger of becoming addicted to the various forms of treatment. One of the advantages of even minor side-effects of drugs and restrictions in diet is that there are positive advantages for the patient when it comes to giving up the treatment once the course has been completed. To those who complain I explain that they are not going to have to take the drugs permanently. Today there are new drugs called tetracyclics, and some of these are easier to take. I am quite sure that we are only at the beginning of drug therapy, and that much more exciting remedies are on the way. Researchers have recently discovered that the body manufactures its own 'animal opiate' called enkephalin, and it is the production of this substance that keeps us most of the time in a physical and mental state of comfortable equalibrium. The utter misery of depression could be because the level of enkephalin has dropped too low. Everyone knows the old story of how toothache can suddenly disappear when one reaches the dentist's consulting room. One explanation of this is that the anxiety of the situation has produced extra enkephalin in the circulation, and it is this that has abolished the pain. We are only at the beginning of our knowledge of the intricacies of brain chemistry.

Lithium Carbonate
The third drug I want to discuss is a simple salt called lithium carbonate. The action of lithium was discovered by an Australian scientist, who had found that guinea pigs fed on most of the urates became hyperactive. However, when he

gave them one of the few soluble salts, lithium urate, no such active mood occurred. His curiosity was aroused, so he gave guinea pigs that had been stimulated by urates lithium carbonate and their activity was soon subdued. He then went on to try the salts of lithium on human patients suffering from manic excitement, and they too rapidly settled down.

Today, lithium is the drug of choice for mania, but what is even more important is that it can even *prevent* attacks from occurring. It can also be most useful with patients suffering from primary endogenous depression who are liable to frequent recurrent attacks. I had a patient who had as many as three attacks a year, and these had gone on over some three decades. Once she was put on continuous lithium therapy the extreme moods settled down, so that she needed no other treatment. Since lithium was started she has had no severe emotional disturbance. Relatives have told me that they are aware of minor mood changes, but these are quite trivial, and she now never needs to report to the doctor because of them.

One of the differences between lithium treatment, and that of the other anti-depressant drugs, is that this salt must be given continuously, and this means that the blood levels need to be monitored. Too little of the drug is ineffective; too much, and it becomes toxic. Signs of toxicity are a tremor of the hands and a raging thirst. To maintain the correct level in the system regular blood tests are necessary, but this sort of discipline is a small price to pay for the prevention of mania or recurrent attacks of depression.

The discovery of psychotropic drugs made as much difference to my work as a G.P. in the control of depressive disorders as did the antibiotics in the realm of the infectious diseases. In suitable cases, the anti-depressant agents work even when the recipient has no faith in their action. One of our nursing sisters, who had severe arthritis, fell and broke her thigh and had to spend a long stretch of time under the orthopaedic surgeon in her own hospital. I visited her socially one day, and I found her in a very angry mood. She admitted that she had been tearful and depressed for some time, but she was infuriated when the surgeon prescribed anti-depressant drugs. Like some others in the caring professions, she thought that depression was a disgraceful type of malady, and she felt that she had been insulted because her doctor had assumed that she could sink so low. However, she had the good sense to do as she was told, and when I saw her two weeks later, things were very different. She told me she was quite amazed to find that a few tablets could make such a difference to her sense of well-being.

Vitamin Deficiencies

When I was a medical student, while discussing the incidence of the various diseases, we were taught that sparrows were much more common than canaries, even if the latter are much more spectacular. The type of melancholia which requires drug treatment, while not as rare as the canary, is certainly not the sparrow of depressive disorders. Many common mild low mood syndromes are due to diets defective in vitamins B and C, but especially the B complex.

Frith,[1] a retired surgeon, helped to conduct an assessment of psychiatric disorders in the general practice of a friend. She reported that some 56 per cent of those patients showed physical evidence of hypovitaminosis B. They all improved when given dried yeast tablets or some vitamin B compound and this improvement was sustained. The medical profession as a whole has overlooked this possible source of mild depression, which is usually labelled a neurosis. Frith herself called her cases neuroses.

In an interesting monograph on vitamins, Marks[2] has described in detail the symptoms of deficiencies of these items worked out on volunteers who were prepared to live for several weeks on diets free from the various vitamins. Let us look at just one example, the effect of a shortage of thiamin (B1). The author observed that mental symptoms appeared long before there were any signs of the defect in other tissues or organs. In listing the actual symptoms they appeared as follows: depression, irritability, failure to concentrate, and a defective memory. Later, items like lack of energy and loss of appetite were mentioned, and of course the last habit could help to perpetuate the syndrome. All these symptoms are classical symptoms of endogenous depression.

Without going into details, shortages of nicotinic acid (B3), pyridoxine (B6), cyanocobalamine (B12) and ascorbic acid,

(C) can produce the same evidence of low moods and wretchedness. Pellagra due to nicotinic acid deficiency is called *mal de la misère* by the French. Premenstrual tension, which is a brief but unpleasant syndrome recurring with every period in some women, can be due to a shortage of pyridoxine. If an adequate dose of this substance is taken well before the menses are due, and continued until it is over, the misery of this syndrome can be relieved in some 50 per cent of cases.

B Complex Deficiency

While I am sure that mild cases of the low mood syndrome are common in avitaminosis, severe cases are rare, but they do occur and the cause is often completely overlooked. Pernicious anaemia is due to a shortage of B12. This illness can now readily be diagnosed because the level of the cyanocobalamine can be measured in the blood, and a low level is diagnostic. Thirty years ago there was no such test and to diagnose the illness the patient had to become anaemic with the typical blood picture of pernicious anaemia (P.A.). A medical colleague's father had died of this illness before there was any treatment for it, and at the age of 50 my friend became vaguely ill. He felt weak, wretched, and was sure he was developing a cancer. P.A. was suspected, but all blood tests and other investigations were negative. After four years of misery he went pale and yellow, and the diagnosis was obvious; he was given B12 and made a rapid recovery.

In my own practice I have had three similar cases. One was given, over a matter of three years, a whole series of psychiatric diagnoses before he became pale and the true cause of his trouble was discovered. With more refined tests, this should not happen today, but I am sure the odd case of severe depression due to the shortage of some vitamin is still missed.

Unlike the treatment with anti-depressant drugs, depression due to avitaminosis clears rapidly once the defect is corrected. Mrs Reed became very miserable and dejected when her husband went off with another woman. She struggled to keep at work, but she became so thin and ill that her sister persuaded her to come and see me. Counselling did little good. She was an intelligent woman and she had tried already to work through her problems; but there was no easy answer. In her trouble she had badly neglected herself. She had lost her appetite, and found that she could get by on very little food. Her skin was dry and flaking. Sleeping alone had been a problem, but this she had solved by taking a nightcap of gin. She was given large doses of vitamins B and C, and advised on her diet. She improved rapidly on this regime and found that she could drop her tot of gin at night. Lack of vitamins had certainly aggravated the symptoms of her reactive depression.

It should be noted that vegetarians who exclude even dairy products from their diet and who never eat any milk derivatives or eggs are particularly vulnerable to B12 shortages. Soya bean products are some of the few sources of this important food factor, but as a precaution it is wise to have an annual blood check on the level of cyanobalamine.

To summarize this last section, and bring the subject into perspective, I suggest that shortages of vitamin B complex are common, and that this can produce a subnormal pattern of health, of which depression is one of the symptoms. Furthermore, in susceptible people, and much more rarely, the victim may well be pushed into a state of severe melancholy.

The Dangers of Tranquillizers

For many years I have hailed the anti-depressant drugs as a great medical advance; but shortly after their introduction, the pharmaceutical houses began to produce some new sedative preparations which were called minor tranquillizers or just tranquillizers. The G.P. was bombarded by attractive advertisements, and we were all told that what the anti-depressants did for melancholia and what the antipsychotic drugs did for schizophrenia, the tranquillizers could do for anxiety and the psychoneuroses. Psychotherapy did indeed take up a lot of the doctor's time and here, we were told, was a quick way of solving our patients' problems.

The idea was attractive and, along with many others, I adopted it for a time. Instead of counselling, patients were given gaily coloured capsules of Librium or Valium. These agents did indeed relieve the symptoms of anxiety, but they also produced a cohort of addicts, and I soon learned that there was no chemotherapeutic short-cut in the treatment of the anxious patient. I gave up the tranquillizers and returned to counselling. Anxiety and depression are basically different emotional reactions. The first is alerting, and the second inhibiting. Fear and its prolonged version anxiety are protective mechanisms and tend to serve a useful purpose. The hiker crossing a field who is chased by a bull, is literally lent wings by his fear reaction, and he will be able to run faster than he has ever done before.

In the same way, anxiety alerts the victim and forces her to seek a solution to her problem. Overwhelming stress may render the patient ill, but the correct solution is to help her to face up to what has happened, and either to solve the problem, or in some way come to terms with it. Merely to damp down useful anxiety by means of drugs is comparable with giving opiates to relieve pain. Pain, like anxiety is a useful red light warning the sufferer of trouble. A pain in the lower abdomen may indicate appendicitis, and so lead to a radical treatment of the condition. Opiates would certainly relieve the pain, but they would also obscure the diagnosis, so that the patient could go on to develop a fatal intra-abdominal infection. Morbid depression on the other hand, is a symptom of an illness, and it demands treatment. If psychotherapy fails, then active treatment is indicated to help restore the delicate emotional balance. The action of anti-depressant agents and tranquillizers are thus quite different.

It is of course, much easier to hand out a prescription for some tablets than to spend twenty minutes listening to a patient's problem. On the other hand, while the tranquillizers may make the patient feel more comfortable, they do not solve the basic problem which is causing the distress. It should be noted that patients on such drugs are to some extent doped all the time and their reactions can become quite abnormal. Let us take the example of a housewife who goes out to work in a factory each day to augment the family income. One day she has a splitting headache and leaves her work early. On reaching home, she finds her husband in bed with the girl from next door. Her normal reaction should be one of aggressive anger, telling the couple what she thinks of them –

perhaps even resorting to physical violence. Doped with tranquillizers, her behaviour could be quite different, passive and strangely illogical. She could only slink away and take an overdose of aspirins.

There *is* a place for the limited use of both tranquillizers and hypnotics. Faced with a sudden calamity, the survivors sometimes need immediate physical help. We made good use of this technique during the Second World War, and heavy sedation could be a great boon to the victim. There is a great deal of individual variation as regards the reaction to all drugs. Even with a sudden bereavement, I do not use sedation indiscriminately. There are, however, people who prefer to work their way through such situations without any drug treatment, and some of course provide their own medication by way of alcohol. If tranquillizers are prescribed, they should only be given for a very limited time (I would suggest a week at the most), and with this proviso there is little risk of patients becoming addicted to the drugs.

Electroplexy (E.C.T.)

Electroplexy or electroconvulsive therapy (E.C.T.) was invented by two Italian psychiatrists in the 1930s, and this treatment was the first form of physical therapy which could rapidly and drastically alter the mood of the patient. Depression cleared and the gross overactivity of the manic patient was damped down. After a course of about six treatments given at the rate of two sessions a week the patient made a recovery and once again assumed normal mood levels. To psychiatrists who were used to watching such patients for months on end, unable to offer any active treatment, the rapid recoveries appeared little short of miraculous. At last they had a tool with which to help many of their unhappy patients. Admittedly, they could not explain how the treatment worked and even today we do not understand the mechanism.

This was no new situation in medicine. Quinine, for instance, was taken to help malarial patients long before anyone knew the mechanism of the process. The early methods of E.C.T. were crude and unpleasant for the patients, but the sick people did improve rapidly, and the duration of the suffering was shortened. Today the treatment has been greatly modified. It is far less unpleasant for the patient, and it is both safe and painless. The sick person is given a prick into a small vein on the back of the hand and rapidly drops off to sleep. Afterwards the patient may have a slight headache, and a few temporary holes in her memory, but these things soon pass. I have known a number of academics who have submitted to this treatment. They have assured me that the memory loss was of short duration and the treatment had in no way impaired their intellectual capacity.

Electroplexy has received a good deal of bad publicity. In the days before chemotherapy was available, E.C.T. was the only procedure available which could offer a rapid relief to depressed people. One man told me he wished he had been offered it months earlier; and others who have had relief have come back and requested more once they felt the clouds of depression descending.

There are times when these measures can heal a broken heart better than any other means of treatment. Mrs Thomson and her husband had a delightful cottage in the country. They owned a beautiful garden with a small artificially made fishpond. One day their two year old son went missing, and he was found drowned in this tiny pond. Mrs Thompson went into a deep depression and blamed herself for allowing such a hazard to exist in the garden. She got more and more miserable, and no amount of listening to her story, or discussing the subject was any help to her. She began to find she was harbouring an illogical hate against her other children because they reminded her of the one she had lost and I advised her that she must have some E.C.T. Six weeks later when I saw her, she was a different person. She could now think more objectively about things, and the sense of self-blame was no longer dominating most of her waking moments. She told me that she had had absolutely no faith in the treatment, but felt that she must give it a trial. This all took place twenty-five years ago, and there has been no relapse.

Electroplexy is only rarely needed for patients today, but under certain circumstances, there is a place for it, and few psychiatrists would care to be denied access to this means of treatment. It has one big advantage over drug therapy: it brings about a recovery more rapidly than the chemical methods. At the end of six weeks Mrs Thomson was completely well. If she had been helped by drugs, she would have had to take them regularly for anything from six months to a year. A problem which can worry the depressed patient about this kind of treatment is that it may be forced upon her. The answer to this is that most psychiatrists are prepared to use their powers of persuasion, but will not compel the patient against her wishes to have the treatment. The only time the patient is given it without her consent is when she is too ill to know what is happening, and those who have reached this nadir generally do very well on the treatment.

The situation is comparable with that of the neurosurgeon who is faced with an unconscious patient in need of an operation to relieve the pressure of a bony fracture on the brain. It would be futile and foolish to wait for the patient's agreement. He collects the consent of the next of kin, and then goes ahead with the life-saving operation. In a similar situation, the psychiatrist must do the same. In such a profound state of depression, or in severe manic excitement, patients have died of the illness. It must be emphasized, once again, that physical treatment, no matter what its nature, needs to be given hand in hand with supportive measures. All along the patient must be made to feel that she is in the hands of someone who understands her and cares for her: someone who respects her as a person.

Notes

[1] K. Frith, *World Medicine*. 10 March 1979.
[2] J. Marks, *The Vitamins*. M.T.P., Lancaster, 1975.

Chapter 7
The Role of Self-help

Nobody realizes, more clearly than members of the medical profession that in almost every sphere of their work things are not perfect; that they are, indeed, capable of being modified and improved. Trends are constantly being reviewed, and every effort is made to enhance contemporary methods of treatment.

When I was a young doctor working in a large maternity hospital we lost something like thirty women a year from complications in childbirth, and the death rate for the country as a whole ran into thousands. The number today for England and Wales is a little over 100, and if a fatal case does occur the whole history of the incident is reviewed by an expert committee to establish the exact cause of death and to see how far this tragic event can be prevented in future problems of that nature.

All who are interested in mental health and depression must adopt the same attitude of healthy criticism of present facilities, to see if better ways can be found to deal with the problem. Over the past forty years great progress has been made in the understanding of depression and in the treatment of the various syndromes, but there is no room for complacency in this vast problem of human misery. There are still some patients who do not get the help they need. The treatment available is not infallible, and the skill of the physicians varies in quality.

Patients naturally find it hard to understand when the help they need is not available from some G.P.s, but the range of skills needed by these physicians is very wide. The man who is unskilled at handling depressed patients may by some skilled diagnosis save another person's life, or he may be an expert at helping to bring healthy babies into this world. This may not be much comfort to the patient who is seeking sympathy and understanding, but I feel that such people should appreciate that this fault lies to some extent in the almost explosive speed of medical progress in this century. The technical side has developed so rapidly and in such a spectacular manner that the caring professions have sometimes, regrettably, been blinded by science to the detriment of medicine as a whole. The idea of listening to a sobbing woman or to a recitation of the vague symptoms of a melancholic does not appeal to all doctors, and some go as far as to say that if they had wanted to do such work they would have opted in the first place for the social services or the church.

Unfortunately, emotional problems cannot be separated from physical illnesses, and a profession dazzled by the success of its scientific progress can miss a very important element in the treatment it offers. A good example of how we have gone adrift in this field is in the care of the cancer patient. Tremendous effort and research has increased the skill in both diagnosis and treatment, but little progress has been made in the art of dealing with the patient's fear and anxiety.

Over the past decade many of us have been helped by the pioneer work of Cicily Saunders, which has revolutionized the care of the terminal cancer patient. There are indeed welcome signs that the tide has turned and that there is a resurgence in the *art* of medicine. Medical schools are now well aware of some of the defects in the training of young doctors in these matters and they are doing their best to redress the situation. In the meantime, in some instances, the sick themselves have joined together to help each other. There is a body called the Cancer Aftercare and Rehabilitation Society (C.A.R.E.),* in which cancer patients and people who have recovered from cancer set out to help others in similar trouble. They are able

* C.A.R.E. Lodge Cottage, Church Lane, Timsbury, Bath.

to talk and explain in a way few doctors or nurses seem able to tackle the problem.

I have already stressed how in the rough and tumble of life, people suffering from neuropsychiatric illnesses fare badly on many counts. They are so often looked down on by neighbours, and they become sensitive to these hostile attitudes, so that they approach their doctor with the greatest diffidence, and are easily rebuffed, maybe by the receptionist before they even reach the G.P. himself. It is because of this that certain self-help societies have grown up to deal with such people.

Depressives Associated

Depressives Associated (D.A.)* is made up of those who have at one time or another suffered from a depressive illness and who wish to share their experiences with fellow sufferers in order to help each other in any way possible. Many D.A. members suggest that unless one has been depressed oneself, one just cannot appreciate the horror of the experience or, indeed, truly sympathize with the victim. While to some extent this is true, as I have already mentioned, there are many like myself who have been dealing with melancholics for so long that we do appreciate just how they suffer; indeed, I have always made a point of stressing that depression is one of the most unpleasant illnesses known to man.

D.A. befriends fellow depressives in a number of ways. My personal point of contact with them was by way of public meetings in big cities. I have been impressed by their sincerity, and enlightened by many of their views. They sometimes meet together in groups to discuss problems, and on other occasions the contact is on a one-to-one basis, or even by letter. Being able to talk to someone who is sympathetic in a way only a fellow sufferer can be is sometimes a source of great comfort. One such patient at the nadir of his depression said that being able to talk by the hour was the only activity that meant anything to him. No doctor or nurse has the time to sit back and offer such facilities whenever they are demanded. They have too many other patients to consider. Peers with only one

* 19 Merley Ways, Wimborne Minster, Dorset, BH21 1QN.

fellow sufferer to befriend can give more time, and in discussions of this kind, they often find common ground, and this can be a great help, as they go on to discover that they are in a sense equals, and very much in the same boat. It should be said, however, that D.A. is generally opposed to E.C.T. treatment and sometimes rejects orthodox medical assistance.

G.R.O.W.

Another organization dealing with these problems sprang up in Australia. Called G.R.O.W.,* its aims are for members to grow up and become mature persons. It describes itself as an association of people who are, or have been, troubled by 'nerves'. In the British Isles, this body has its headquarters in Ireland and at the time of writing it does not appear yet to have crossed the Celtic Sea. Members of the group meet weekly, the size of the circle being limited to about ten, to discuss mutual problems. They take it in turns to chair meetings, which tend to last for two hours, and the discussion ends over a friendly cup of tea.

This body has certain quite clear objectives outlined in what they call the twelve steps of G.R.O.W., and they have clarified their ideas for thinking objectively into a set of well-defined rules. The meetings are quite informal. Members make use of their own experience, and they take advantage of any other help available. They do, when necessary, work closely with the medical profession. If drugs have been prescribed by the doctor, then this regime is accepted, even if at times it is questioned. Co-operation with the psychiatric services is maintained. Members of a group are always encouraged to befriend each other between meetings, by telephone, letters or face to face contacts. Anything that will draw the sick person into companionship with the group is encouraged so that one by one the twelve steps to maturity are mounted.

The whole point of their work is to help the patient understand herself and to develop the self-discipline which comes from within. Joannie was a chronic schizophrenic who

---

* G.R.O.W., 209a Edgeware Road, Marrickville, N.S.W. 2204, Australia. G.R.O.W., 26 Paul Street, Cork City, Ireland.

had spent many years in a psychiatric hospital after a breakdown at the age of nineteen. Her parents got in touch with G.R.O.W. and the group took an interest in her. She came to the meetings a rejected hopeless schizophrenic, unable to co-operate with anyone at first; but slowly and patiently she was befriended and drawn into the circle, and over a period of five years she learned, with their help, the difficult art of self-rehabilitation. For some years now she has been at work, self-supporting in every way. She has joined the staff of G.R.O.W. in Australia as an international group leader. The story of her life makes exciting reading,[1] and offers hope to many people suffering from chronic mental handicaps of any kind, including long-standing depressions. There *is* a way out of the maelstrom.

Group Therapy,

Group therapy is no new idea. It has been organized by the psychiatric and social services for a very long time, and such groups have helped many people to a better understanding of themselves and their problems. However, there is a paternalistic, authoritarian atmosphere about study circles started in this way. There is a different, freer and perhaps more tolerant attitude among peer groups. The former type is in some way reminiscent of a school, with a teacher in charge, even if he keeps as far as possible in the background. No matter how he tries, a sense of inferiority may silence those who are supposed to be talking.

The appeal of belonging to a small group of equals can, I think, be explained in the history of our species. For something like two million years mankind lived in small groups. At first they wandered across the earth as hunter-gatherers, and some ten thousand years ago, as early farmers, they lived in small village communities, a situation that remained until the Industrial Revolution a mere two hundred years ago. Then began the great migration of humanity to the towns. In evolutionary terms, this new way of life is a habit acquired overnight, and the old life has not yet been totally forgotten. Today, man has to live as an isolated unit in a vast community, but he is still a great deal happier in a small group of people he knows well and who are his equals, as were the villagers of byegone days. The togetherness and the sense of belonging helped them to survive hardships. Thus, man is instinctively glad to return to a way of life he enjoyed for some two million years of pre-history. Self-help groups, in a way, recreate this almost forgotten society, with all the benefits that accrued from it.

New Psychiatric Techniques

Psychiatric workers are not blind to the need to look for new ways of tackling the apparently incurable cases. For example there is some interesting work being done among the chronic mentally sick in South Africa. There are now some seven units where intensive care and a great deal of personal enthusiasm is focused on patients who are virtually the rejects of the state mental hospitals. On admission the patients can be described as hopeless, for they have certainly given up all hope and have ceased to care for themselves in any way. They are often depraved and are all very sick.

These unpromising patients are put into small groups with a high nurse-patient ratio and given a great deal of individual attention. Care of personal hygiene, toilet habits and appearance are all encouraged, and activities of all kinds are organized for most of the day. Marks are allotted to group members for good co-operation and for keeping to simple rules of behaviour. Improvement means promotion to a higher grade and this is rewarded by all kinds of privileges, which encourages further progress. Slowly the patients move up to the top grades where they can do real work round the hospital with a minimum of supervision. The net result is a laudable discharge rate back to normal life and work in the community of a number of patients who had been abandoned as hopeless, and this experiment showed to me just what dedication and enthusiasm of the caring professions can do.

I have already spoken of the Industrial Revolution which virtually drove the peasant communities into the towns. Another comparable change took place in the life of Western man soon after the Second World War. For the first time in the history of the human race, the common man was able to live in comparative affluence, and he had time for leisure pursuits and holidays which have become ever more exotic. It was assumed that the National Health Service would so improve the basic well-being of the community that the cost of medicine would diminish, and that the number of hospital beds could be drastically cut. This has not happened, indeed quite the reverse situation has arisen. The national health bill rises year by year; the waiting list for hospital beds gets longer and longer, and new and bigger hospitals are demanded.

Modern Failures

Unfortunately, wealth and health do not go hand in hand. The doctors have indeed largely conquered the infectious disease, but in terms of positive health, we are failing abysmally. Something like 40 per cent of people in Scotland over fourteen years of age have no teeth of their own. Developing African races do far better than that. Countless men in the very prime of life die of heart disease, and the blame for this lies in part in the bad habits we have acquired of over-eating, combined with a lack of proper exercise. Positive health cannot be imposed on people by supplying a health service, or by giving good wages, better housing and longer holidays. The urge for achieving good health must come from within.

We are all of us in need of a great deal of internal discipline. It is obvious that if our brain cells are to function properly they must have the essential ingredients they need, and these must come from the food we take into our bodies. Today the trend is to eat refined materials, often artificially coloured to attract attention, and preserved either by chemicals added to each item, or by way of the deep freeze. We have gone far away from eating a healthy balanced diet, and as a result of this we tend to put on weight and suffer from constipation, rheumatism of the hips and knees, and a varying degree of avitaminosis. We add to the artificiality of life by driving everywhere in a car and breathing lead-laden fumes. Regular exercise of our muscles is all but forgotten. These tendencies must be reversed, and self-help for the patient recovering from a depression must include a rule of life attending to these things.

The Importance of Diet

Experiments have shown that good food can make all the difference to the quality of life. In one piece of research a group of delinquent girls, who had been living on white bread and margarine, cheap jam, sweet tea and processed foods, were taken into a hostel where their diet was changed to one which included wholemeal bread, fresh fruit, fresh meat and vegetables from the garden. Not only did they begin to look better and physically more attractive, but they were less quarrelsome and many of their bad habits faded away.

Everyone benefits from a sensible diet. With a reasonable helping of bran mixed in with breakfast cereals nobody need be constipated. Vegetables must be cooked with great care so as not to destroy the vitamin content. Buy them as fresh as possible and prepare them immediately before cooking. Do not soak them. In the cooking process, both the time and the amount of water used should be kept to a minimum. Salads are better for us than most cooked vegetables. Many items ordinarily cooked, like carrots, celery and cabbage, can be eaten raw with enjoyment. Attention to the quality of the food is good for the housewife in two ways. It is better nutritionally, and it gives her a greater interest in the preparation of food.

Exercise

Exercise in some form should be as much a part of the daily routine as eating. If you are the energetic type you can take up squash or tennis, but even walking is good for you, though to be effective this needs to be brisk. The longer you walk, the better, but even half an hour is helpful. A leisurely stroll along the promenade at the seaside cannot be classified as exercise, nor can the gentle pottering about her housework by an overweight woman. Exercise should be brisk enough to raise the heart rate and to make the individual a little breathless, but there should be enough puff left to carry on a conversation. Only by activities of this kind can the heart muscle be extended to capacity and the lungs fully inflated each day. Above all, exercise should be regular, every day if possible, and regulated to the capacity of the individual.

Yoga exercises are excellent from this point of view. They are not violent, but at the same time they are designed to use muscles to the fullest extent possible for each individual, and to extend that person's capacity by practice. Concentration is necessary for co-ordination, and this is good for the mind as well as the body. Classes are held in a pleasant and relaxed atmosphere and may well provide a very congenial group which can be of great help to all people under stress.

This is of particular use to the recovering melancholic. At the nadir of her depression she has little appetite for either food or exercise. She just wants to sit about, or creep back into bed. This is not unreasonable at the very start of treatment, especially if there is someone to look after the house; but as soon as the clouds begin to lift the effort must be made to follow a healthy routine. Obviously this cannot be done all at once, but she should seek to acquire a workable rule of life, compatible with her energy reserves. No matter how much bed attracts in the morning, she must force herself to get up at the right time. A rest at midday may be allowed, but lying down all the time is to be avoided.

Care must be taken with personal hygiene. A man certainly feels cleaner and better for a good shave. The same applies to women in their attention to the rituals of make-up. Meals should be taken at regular intervals, even if the appetite is at a low ebb. The patient should make sure that she at least eats the nourishing parts of the meals, and does not allow herself to nibble biscuits and drink tea all day. Added vitamins in tablet form may help her appetite. Alcohol should be avoided, or taken only in modest amounts. It is all too easy to become dependent on the repeated drink, and many a melancholic has become an alcoholic once it has been discovered that this readily available drug can to some extent ease the agony of depression. Fresh air and exercise are most important, although the severely depressed person may have little interest in either. She should be encouraged to take a few deep breathes as she has a short wander round the garden.

Such simple rules may seem hard at the time, but they are important both for physical health and for the patient's morale. A small success in keeping to one of her rules means a triumph for her will power, and a rise in her sense of self-esteem – something which is in urgent need of a boost. Once recovery has set in, the brakes may have to be applied. The patient should be careful not to overdo things. She still needs to adhere to sensible hours for rest. Parties which go on until two in the morning are not a good idea for the recovering patient. She must try to progress through her convalescence just as she would if she were recovering from a severe chest infection, or an operation.

Dependence on Drugs

Besides the deplorable popularity of processed foods we have also become a nation of pill takers. As Peregrine Worsthorne once put it:

> The truth is that the phenomenal expansion of drug swallowing in recent years carries with it a new social danger. Once upon a time only the very sick put themselves at risk by the taking of drugs. Today, only the very healthy do without them. People demand drugs for the slightest indisposition.[2]

The doctors as well as the laity are responsible for this curious state of affairs. A girl of sixteen may start taking the contraceptive pill. If she happens to live in America she may be expected to take hormone replacement therapy at the menopause. One gynaecologist told me he stopped such treatment when the patient had reached eighty-six! The unfortunate woman could have embarked soon after puberty on some seventy years of pill taking. When patients attend a doctor they expect to be given some physical remedy, and I often sensed that the patient whose troubles we had discussed for half an hour still felt she wanted some tangible proof of my interest in her. In the correct amount in the right patient, medicaments do help, but all of us tend to expect too much of them, and we take too many.

A woman of thirty-two came to see me because she was depressed. There seemed to be no external basis for her feelings, but on taking her history I found she was on the contraceptive pill. I suggested for a start, she should come off the pill and adopt some other method of birth control. When I saw her a month later all her depressive symptoms had gone, and it was clear that the tablets had been the basis of her trouble. I do not think this is a common cause of depression,

but it may happen more often than we realize. A friend of
mine was under treatment for her high blood pressure, which
was affecting her heart. She was greatly restricted in her
activities, and she became more and more miserable and
depressed – a housebound invalid unable to do even the
simplest chores. Her blood pressure responded well to the
treatment, but she herself felt a great deal worse. After months
of misery, her doctor decided to stop all her tablets for a few
weeks. In no time she was a great deal better, and it was
obvious that one or more of her medicaments was at fault.
This factor was identified, another drug was substituted for it,
and she continued to feel well.

Food Allergies

Just as some people react adversely to drugs that do not upset
other people, so others react to items of food which are usually
quite innocuous. In other words, the individual may have
some food allergy. The main target area for allergy is the skin.
The person who comes out in a rash after eating strawberries
or shellfish can usually spot very easily the cause of the
trouble, especially if it is a reaction to something which is
eaten only occasionally. If, however, the noxious agent is
something constantly taken in the diet, it becomes more
difficult to locate the allergen. For many years now it has been
recognized that people suffering from coeliac disease can
remain well as long as they avoid food containing the
substance gluten, which occurs in wheat flour. Adults
contracting this allergy start to lose weight, have bulky
offensive stools and feel generally unwell. Once the cause of
the trouble has been spotted, and they go onto a gluten-free
diet, all their symptoms vanish. In much the same way there
are victims of infantile eczema who are rapidly relieved of their
symptoms by switching from cow's to goat's milk.

The syndromes I have just described, have clear-cut
physical signs. Sometimes, however, the allergy consists of
vague symptoms, and a general lowering in the quality of life.
An example of this was the young woman who was allergic to
the contraceptive pill, which brought on depressive symptoms.
If the symptoms are minor and the patient merely feels a little
below par, this kind of sensitivity may be difficult to spot. I

America a great deal of work has been done on this subject which is called masked food sensitivity or allergy. The patient is reacting to common everyday food items such as some cereal, milk, eggs, tea or coffee. The target organ is not shown up by a rash or a streaming nose, but the patient is afflicted by a vague sub-standard level of health and perhaps feelings of dissatisfaction with life and with depression. The way to locate such a sensitivity is to omit all suspected food items from the diet for five days. During this period withdrawal symptoms can occur, but after five days there is usually a dramatic rise in morale and a consequent feeling of well-being. The causative agent can then be excluded from the diet in the future. A young executive found in this way that he was sensitive to the caffeine in tea and coffee. Dropping these items made him feel a great deal better.

Sometimes it is not the basic foods that cause allergic reactions but the preservatives and colouring matter introduced by the manufacturers to make their products look more attractive. Dramatic improvement has been claimed in the behaviour of over-active children when these items have been carefully excluded from the diet. In such cases it is clear that these factors were affecting the brain and causing the overactivity, in much the same way as urates hyper-excite guinea pigs (see page 95).

Failure to Respond to Treatment
The vast majority of depressed patients can be helped back to normality. This may be by way of counselling, by changing the environment, or by altering the brain chemistry. The latter may be affected by the addition of some missing factor such as insulin for the diabetic, nicotinic acid for the pellagrin, or thyroid for the patient whose body cannot manufacture this essential hormone. Other patients are helped by taking drugs which are able to adjust the balance of the emotional control centre which is temporarily out of order, and here I am referring to the anti-depressant drugs. Others are improved by the exclusion of food or drug items which are having an adverse effect on the emotional controls.

Unfortunately, there are still a few people in whom the basis of the depression remains exasperatingly elusive. Mrs Vickers has been an awkward prickly character ever since her early teens. She was so disruptive in the home that the family heaved a sigh of relief when she took on a job in Leicester and found rooms in the city. She soon fell foul of her landlady and then she began a long trek from one place to another. She somehow found a long-suffering boy friend and they were married, but she still continued to fall out with most people. After a few months of marriage, she became pregnant and an entirely new personality emerged. She was quite a different person, happy and contented as she looked forward to the birth of her child. She had an easy confinement, but two weeks later she broke down into a severe depressive illness, and she was so disturbed she had to be referred to a psychiatric unit. She had the only treatment then available, which was E.C.T. She recovered, but on her return home she was her old irritable self. She never dared to have another child, being so appalled by the depression she had experienced.

Years later I asked her what had been the happiest time of her life, and without a moment's hesitation she said it was when she was carrying her child. The mixture of hormones in circulation when she was pregnant had given her a sense of tranquillity we were not able to reproduce by any form of replacement therapy then available, but clearly there must have been some chemical basis for the dramatic change in her moods and way of life.

A similar case had a happier ending. The patient was a married woman of forty-eight with three fine sons, and for eight years she had suffered from a multitude of vague complaints for which there was no clear-cut explanation. A great deal of time was spent on counselling and she was referred to a number of consultants, but nobody seemed able to solve her problem. It was when she was forty-eight that she reported with pelvic symptoms, and it was clear that she had reached the menopause. An examination revealed that she was short of certain items and hormone replacement therapy was initiated. From then on she was very much better, and only came to the surgery to collect a new supply of tablets. After three years these were tailed off and she remained well. This woman, like Mrs Vickers, had some hormonal imbalance which was not located for eight years, and then by a stroke of luck she was given the correct mixture which returned her to normal health. Many are less fortunate and continue on a sub-normal level of health.

Therapists of all kinds have a failure rate. We cannot always locate the vital factor or supply what is really needed. Unfortunately, some patients who could be helped are put off from seeking the treatment they need by sheer mismanagement. The patient who is handed a box of the latest anti-depressant tablets, without any explanation of what she can expect by way of side-effects, may become so ill after a few doses she may well feel that the cure is worse than the disease. She thus remains in a state of depression when a little understanding and an adjustment of the dosage could well have given real relief. On the other hand, the patient herself may have slipped into bad habits which she needs to correct, and to do this she may need the support of some therapist or some self-help organization. It has also to be said that some patients do not always accept the help that is offered to them.

Having located someone who is prepared to help, and whom the patient feels she can trust, every effort must be made to make the relationship work. Some people question every piece of advice they are given. This is a non-productive attitude. The patient should listen to what her advisor suggests, even if she cannot see the point of it. To go shopping around from one helper to another can be a complete waste of time for all concerned.

Let us suppose the patient seeks help from the social services, and she is allocated to some worker who is prepared to listen to her problems in an attempt to sort things out together. The sick person must attend each session as advised, and she must make a point of getting there on time. If she does not agree with something, she has every right to speak her mind, indeed she *must* do so. But even if there is some disagreement she must see the treatment through. This applies even when things seem to be going slowly. As we have seen, psychotherapy is a two-way process: it is more than a pleasant social chat. The process of probing and questioning can be painful, and the patient is frequently upset by the exploration of the sensitive area. She may seek to deny some problem, or even pretend that it does not exist. But improvement can only take place when the cards are clearly on the table.

Mrs Fletcher tried hard to persuade herself that the lump in her mother's breast was not a cancer. She did her best not to think about it, and she just could not bring herself to discuss it with either her G.P. or the psychiatrist. It was only when, in a very roundabout way, the real trouble was located that she could get the help she needed, and so come to terms with the situation. The person with some worry which for some reason she does not wish to disclose is like someone in a swimming pool who insists on hiding a water-polo ball by keeping it well down in the water. This can be done for quite a long time, but it requires a constant effort which is extremely exhausting.

There may be other difficulties. If the social worker feels that a psychiatric opinion is needed, then this advice should be followed, no matter how reluctant the patient is. The social worker, after all, has nothing to gain by the referral, and it is done solely for the patient's own good. If drugs are prescribed as a result of such a step, they must be taken as directed. Any discomfort caused by treatment will soon pass if the patient holds firm, and she must remind herself that a temporary inconvenience is well worth enduring in order to get back to a normal state of health. In depression, patients tend to despise themselves for being weak and feeble, and they cannot believe that in health they were hard working, kindly, industrious people, the very salt of the earth. They need to be constantly reminded of this, even if they cannot appear to accept it at the time.

A wise psychiatrist once said to me that the best form of treatment was the one which enabled the patient eventually to stand on her own feet, and be completely independent of drugs, doctors and social workers. It may be a long, hard road, but it can be done. This, finally, is the objective we must all aim to achieve.

Notes

[1] G.R.O.W. Magazine. No. 4, 1975.
[2] *Sunday Telegraph.*

Glossary

Delusion. A false belief not susceptible to argument or reason.

Hypnotic. A drug which induces a sleep-like state of oblivion; a sleeping tablet.

Hypochondriasis. A disorder in which the patient is obsessed by ideas of ill-health, for which there is no physical explanation.

Insight. The patient's ability to appreciate the extent and nature of the illness.

Phobia. An intractable fear which the patient knows is foolish or unreasonable, but cannot escape it.

Psychoneurosis, or neurosis. A condition in which there are faulty emotional responses to the stresses of life. There are various forms including the anxiety state, and this can be combined with depression. This latter is synonymous with a reactive depression.

Psychosis. This is a mental illness in which the patient is badly disturbed, and usually lacks insight into the trouble.

Schizophrenia. A serious mental disorder in which there is an impaired relationship with reality, and sometimes there is a slow disintegration of the personality.

Addresses

C.A.R.E. (Cancer Aftercare and Rehabilitation Society)
Lodge Cottage
Church Lane
Timsbury
Bath

Depressives Associated
19 Merley Ways
Wimborne Minster
Dorset BH21 1QN

G.R.O.W.
26 Paul Street
Cork
Eire

Further Reading

Anthony Horden. *Tranquillity Denied*, Rigby Ltd., 1976.
   A treatise on stress and its impact on the world today.

Richard Mackarness. *Not All In The Mind*, Pan, 1976.
   A study of how unsuspected food allergies can effect the body and the mind.

Colin Murray Parkes. *Bereavement*, Penguin, 1975.
   Studies of grief in adult life.

David Robinson and Stuart Henry. *Self-Help and Health*, Martin Robertson, 1977.
   A comprehensive study of mutual aid for modern problems.

Margaret Torrie. *Begin Again*, Dent, 1970.
   Guidance for women who have been widowed.

C.A.H. Watts. *Depression: Understanding A Common Problem*, Teach Yourself Books, 1975.
   A book on depression aimed at general practitioners, social workers and paramedical staff, but easily understood by the lay public.

Roger J. Williams. *Nutrition Against Disease*, Bantam, 1973.
   A study in environmental prevention of illness by way of an adequate diet.

Index